0.99

CONTEMPORARY
LITERARY
THEORY
AND THE
READING
OF POETRY

CONTEMPORARY LITERARY THEORY

AND THE READING OF POETRY

DAVID BUCHBINDER
Curtin University of Technology, Western Australia

with a chapter on Poetry and Gender by
B A R B A R A H . M I L E C H

M

1060312 3

First published 1991 by
THE MACMILLAN COMPANY OF AUSTRALIA PTY LTD
107 Moray Street, South Melbourne 3205
6 Clarke Street, Crows Nest 2065

Associated companies and representatives
throughout the world

National Library of Australia
cataloguing in publication data

Buchbinder, David, 1947-
    Contemporary literary theory and the reading of poetry.
    Includes index.   0333570243
    ISBN 0 7329 0509 5.
    ISBN 0 7329 0508 7 (pbk.).

    1. Poetry – History and criticism. I. Milech, Barbara H.
    II. Title
809.1

Set in Berkeley Old Style & Novarese Book by
Superskill Graphics, Singapore
Printed in Hong Kong

Contents

Preface

'Another text on literary theory?' I hear the reader murmur. 'Surely the earth already groans under the weight of existing books on the subject.' It is certainly true that in the last decade or so we have witnessed an unparalleled growth in the development of various theories and in the attendant production of all kinds of books about them: explaining them, applying them, extending them.

The proliferation of theories and theoretical schools has had several consequences for the student of English literature. One of these has been a dizzying succession of theories and politico-theoretical positions in the academies. Connected with this, moreover, is the verbal density and difficulty of many of these theories, frequently producing in the student-reader despair at the very idea of ever fully mastering them.

The displacement from the current centre of scholarly theoretical focus of Anglo-American New Criticism, which has dominated school curricula for more than half a century, has had a further consequence for the literature student. There has been a shift in emphasis from the poetic text — the preferred New Critical object of analysis — to the narrative, dramatic or filmic one. A result of this has been the thinning out from many publishers' catalogues of the sort of texts made familiar by the domination of New Criticism: collections both of theoretical essays, and of articles demonstrating the methodology of 'practical criticism' or 'close reading'.

The present volume emerges, then, from several perceived needs of the student of literature. In the first instance, it presents in outline some half-a-dozen current theories or theoretical 'schools'. However, because, as is stressed throughout, none of the theories here presented can be taken as unified and monolithic, the book does not attempt to make itself responsible for every aspect of each theory. Nor, as I have remarked in Chapter 1, is it intended that it replace the many excellent collections of theoretical essays, or the many studies of contemporary theory currently available. Rather, it is hoped that this book will complement them.

It should, moreover, complement them in a particular way. Where these collections and studies deal in a fairly general and perhaps abstract way with theory, or may apply theory to texts other than poetry, this book addresses the specific question of how particular theories produce certain kinds of reading of poems. The poems have been chosen for such application of theory, according to several criteria. These include, first, brevity, not only because it is conducive to the clearer and more compact demonstration of the relevant theory, but also because longer poems tend to move towards, if not, indeed, into narrative, thereby creating a shift in reading and theoretical attention. However, longer poems have not been neglected: the narrative potential of longer poetry is here represented by Carroll's 'Jabberwocky', which provides the exemplary text in the chapter on structuralist theory, while that on poetry and gender also focuses on a longer poem, by Emily Dickinson.

A second criterion is the relative familiarity of the sample poems (and/or of their authors): obscure works might be adjudged deliberately sought out as special cases appropriate to the illustration of the working of a particular theory. The poems (and the poets) included in this book, are, therefore, readily to be found in standard collections and anthologies. Readers outside Australia, however, may not be familiar with Douglas Stewart's poem, 'The Brown Snake', treated in the chapter on Russian Formalism, though it, too, is included in a standard anthology, *The Penguin Book of Australian Verse*.

Third, familiar and recognisable poetic forms were deemed preferable to more irregular or experimental ones. This explains the relatively frequent appearance of sonnets as sample poems (in Chapters 2, 4 and 6), which further allows a certain continuity throughout the volume, so that a variety of comments may be made from several theoretical positions on the sonnet as a particular poetic *form*.

If the chapter on Russian Formalism seems to stress the historical background somewhat more than others, this is because both the history and the theory of Russian Formalism still remain comparatively unknown, even though a number of recent surveys of contemporary literary theory include references to Formalist theory. Though some of the writing of the Formalists has been translated into English over the last decade or so, much more remains untranslated. Being unacquainted with Russian and other Slavic languages, I have relied on the work of such scholars as Victor Erlich to provide a more complete picture of Russian Formalism than the current set of translations might afford.

The chapter on poetry and gender is contributed by my friend and colleague Barbara H. Milech, whose encouragement and advice during the gestation of the present work were invaluable. Her familiarity with current gender theory far outstrips my own, making her the preferred author of this chapter.

Acknowledgements

I would like to acknowledge the support of all my colleagues in the School of Communication and Cultural Studies at Curtin University of Technology, in particular Ross Bennett, Ann McGuire and Margaret Macintyre, who patiently acceded to my several requests to read the various drafts through which this book has passed. Equally patiently, they lent me books from their own libraries and offered me helpful advice, both on the theories dealt with, and on questions of style and rhetoric.

This book appeared in 1987 in a short form under the imprint of Curtin University of Technology. I would like to thank the University for waiving its claim to copyright over the book. The referencing used in this version is that of the Modern Language Association, and links page numbers given parenthetically in the text to the Suggestions for Further Reading at the end of each chapter.

Last, but by no means least, I wish to acknowledge the patience and interest of my poetry students over the years, with special thanks to two former students of note and ability, Jene Lloyd Myles and Sarah Sheppard, with whom, over many cups of coffee, I have discussed various matters of theoretical import. They always managed to provoke and challenge me, to ask probing questions, and to make enlightening comments.

Poetry quoted in the Text

The authors and publisher would like to thank the following for their permission to use copyright material:

Collins/Angus & Robertson on behalf of Margaret Stewart ©, for Douglas Stewart, 'The Brown Snake', from *Collected Poems 1937–1967*, 1967.

Harvard University Press for Emily Dickinson, Poem 640 ('I cannot live without You'), from *The Complete Poems*, ed. Thomas H. Johnson, 1975.

Holt, Rinehart and Winston, on behalf of the Estate of Robert Frost, for Robert Frost, 'Design', from *The Poetry of Robert Frost*, ed. Edward Connery Lathem, 1969.

Oxford University Press, for Sir Philip Sidney, Sonnet 30, from *Astrophil and Stella*, ed. William A. Ringler, Jr., 1962.

Random Century Ltd, on behalf of the Estate of Robert Frost, for Robert Frost, 'Design', from *The Poetry of Robert Frost*, ed. Edward Connery Lathem, 1971.

1
Poetry and Theory

Many of us, when confronted with a poem, suspect that the text is going to be hard to understand, if not, indeed, completely opaque. Thus, we may reject poetry out of hand, even though, in reading other kinds of texts, we may in fact undertake processes as difficult as the ones involved in making meaning in poetic texts.

The presupposition of difficulty arises from a combination of assumptions: first, that the *language* of poetry is itself difficult, and, second, that there is concealed somewhere in this difficult language a 'message' that is invisible to the naked eye. Naturally, it would be vain to deny that poetic language often *is* difficult: only doggerel and greeting card verse are normally and regularly written in easy-to-grasp language. Even so, we can, with care and application, make our way through the verbal structures of a poem with relative confidence, if not with outright ease. One way to do this is to familiarise ourselves with the appropriate theories of literature.

The idea that there is a 'message' buried in the language raises rather different questions. It supposes that the poet had something to say that he or she could have said in plain, simple prose, but chose instead — wilfully, perhaps — to conceal it in decorative and distracting language, rather like those children's puzzles which ask you to count the number of dogs or faces hidden in the picture. Contemporary literary theory, however, argues that the meaning, the 'message', is in fact made *in* and *out of* the text. That is, meaning doesn't exist before the text itself comes into existence, but is *created* by the text. Had the poet written other words into the text, the meaning of the poem would be different *in essence*, not merely in decoration. According to this kind of theory, the reader comes to share responsibility for meaning in the text, since it is his or her activity in reading it that produces meaning.

Before we consider the several contemporary theories discussed in this book, we should ask the following important questions:

Why is it necessary to know anything about literary theory in order to be able to read poetry?

What can we expect a theory to do in its explication of the structures and dynamics of literature in general, and poetry in particular?

Which theory or theories should we adopt?

Why is Theory Necessary?

We often assume that there is a 'natural' way to read, which familiarity with theory can make more sophisticated, on the one hand, or, on the other, which theory might change or complicate unnecessarily. However, the way we read seems natural to us only because it is the way we were taught. If we know of no other ways, we cannot help assuming that ours is the 'natural,' or 'only,' or 'best' way of reading texts.

But if we think about it, we realise that, however we may have been taught to read, our particular method makes certain assumptions about the *text* to be read, and about how important *authors* are to the meaning of the work. Their intention when they wrote, their biographies, and the historical context, all bear on the second.

Our method also makes assumptions about how important *readers* are to the meaning of the work. How readers feel about the text while reading it; how much they know about authors and their times; and what abilities with language readers may possess, are all important. Further, it can make claims about the *historical or social context* of the work and/or of the reader; about *why* we read literary texts, and their relation to other kinds of texts; about the *function* and *importance* of *literature*, and so on. These assumptions and claims are often hidden from us as we go about the business of reading, and it is their concealment that creates the effect of the naturalness of the practice of reading.

Theories of literature are theories about how we read literary texts. They, too, make assumptions about these texts, but talk explicitly of them. They may put forward hypotheses concerning the nature of literary texts, make claims about their value of such texts, or the way in which they should be read. Knowing about such theories identifies for us the way in which we, as individuals, read. From them, we can learn the strengths and weaknesses of a particular practice of reading. And they can offer alternative reading practices which make different meanings in the text that we may find interesting, desirable or useful.

The answer to our question, then, is that, in finding out about literary theories, we also find out what we read *for*. When someone says, 'I read for pleasure' or 'I read to escape', each statement contains an implicit theory about reading and about literature. It suggests that a particular attitude towards literature will, in fiction, foreground narrative or plot, for example, or rhythm in poetry. It will background other concerns, such as historical context or the biography of the author, in order to promote an emotional, chiefly non-analytic response from the reader. The text's 'meaning' will depend on the degree of pleasure felt by the reader.

Exactly the same work, read by another reader with different assumptions and a different theory, will produce another 'meaning'. Take, for instance, a reader for whom the meaning of texts is related to issues in the historical context. To such a person, the degree of pleasure obtained from reading the work is secondary, or even irrelevant, to seeing how the work reflects or relates to events occurring at the time it was written. The same is true of a reader for whom the author's biography and psychology are important. Here, the text is a way to understand the author, which becomes its meaning.

What Can a Theory Do?

What we now need to consider is how a theory explains the functions and inter-relationships of different aspects of the text, and how these guide us towards a particular kind of reading.

Any literary theory has to account for the elements we have already discussed, as well as others. These concern the *nature of representation* in the text; the nature of reality and its relation to representation; how the representation of reality is accomplished or subverted and denied; what conventions or codes particular writers, literary 'schools' or periods might employ to achieve representation.

Another element is the *function* of the literary text in social and cultural terms, which in turn leads to a consideration of its *value*. Literary theory also addresses questions of what makes literary language *literary*, as well as the *structures* of literary language and literary texts, and how these work. Theories foreground these concerns in various ways, but all make certain assumptions about each aspect.

Thus even if, like Plato, theorists think that literature is worthless and should be done away with, their theories need to explain literature in particular ways. In Plato's case, what the theory did was insist that true value lies in reality, not in its representation. Given this central tenet, theory can dispose of such matters as the style of writing and the form of the work by saying that these merely increase representationality, but not reality, in the text. The theme or 'message' that the literary text might contain is thus subordinated to the point almost of irrelevance, because it is embedded in representation, not reality. Questions about the historical or biographical context are also made irrelevant, since Plato's idea of reality is that it is universal and unchanging. Details of the author's life or of historical events, have to do with things that change and are individual, not universal, so these cannot be real or true, according to Plato's definition. In the end, literature is made to seem not only worthless, but dangerous, especially to those who read only for pleasure.

Other theories may prefer certain *kinds* of literature to others. In newspapers, one often reads attacks on particular literary forms or preoccupations — for example, pornographic writing — asserting the morally adverse effect such forms or themes have on, particularly, young readers. Setting aside the question of whether this is true or even likely, we can see that the underlying theory sets up a hierarchy of kinds of literary work, which defines some as 'good' and others as 'bad'. The criterion is moral, not formal or conceptual: that is, what is at issue here is the effect on members of society, not whether the individual work is well written, or whether it says something worth saying. This theory sees literature as a phenomenon capable of affecting society, and not as a mere pastime or as material to think about. Thus, works possessing certain qualities may be classified as 'good' because harmless. If they possess others, they can be stigmatised as 'dangerous'.

One key element in most theories is the way in which the language of literature — and, for our purposes, of poetry in particular — is defined in relation to the other kinds of language current in the culture. Some theories privilege literary language, asserting its difference from, and in some cases, its superiority to, the language of everyday usage. Other theories minimise the differences, though it is conceded that literary language is somehow different from everyday usage. In practice, we don't usually read a novel the same way in which we read a newspaper story, but where some theorists would maintain that this is because the very language of the literary work is different — that it is 'heightened', 'rendered new', or 'made difficult' — others would say that the languages of literature and journalism are simply located at different points along a linguistic spectrum, and that certain conventions of cultural origin encourage us to read these languages differently. After all, we *could* read a newspaper story as fiction, or, if it were reset typographically, as a poem; its meaning would then change. In other words, some theories maintain that the language of literature is different in essence, whereas others argue that its difference lies in the approach of the reader to the text, and the expectations generated by this.

Michael Riffaterre defines the poem as something which 'says one thing and means another'.[1] He goes on to elaborate this notion by identifying these two different kinds of signification in the poem as, first, the representation of reality, *mimesis* (2), and, second, the organisation of elements within the text into signifying systems, *semiosis* (4). Thus, the surface meaning of the poetic text apparently refers to a reality outside itself. Attention to the text itself, however, reveals that it is a self-sustaining structure, compounded of various elements which enable the reader to arrive at a meaning in the poem that has no necessary relationship to any reality outside it.

This distinction between the signifying levels of a poetic text is probably not new to you as a reader of poetry. Even a novice reader is aware that the meaning of a poem (unless extraordinarily simple) is often elusive and slippery, strongly suggesting that what the poem says is not necessarily what it *means*. However, Riffaterre's use of the terms mimesis and semiosis is useful in enabling us to focus on the particular preoccupations of the different theories of reading, and their practices.

We may use Riffaterre's notion to define theories in the following way. *Mimetic theories* are those which insist on the relation of the poetic text to biographical, historical, social and economic realities *outside* the text. *Semiotic theories* foreground the text and its signifying structures, minimising those extrinsic factors which are important to the mimetic theories. This is, of course, an arbitrary and over-simplified differentiation. Practitioners of mimetic theories also frequently begin with a semiotic reading of the poetic text in order to proceed to a discussion of the ways in which the text represents reality. Likewise, semiotic critics have been known to draw on such mimetic elements as historical and cultural context in making sense of the poems under discussion. However, the distinction between mimetic and semiotic functions serves as a way of indicating not an exclusive theoretical concern, but rather a general orientation.

The various theoretical positions regarding literature represent variations in a particular *discourse*. The meaning of this term in theoretical writing tends to be somewhat elastic. For our purposes, however, it refers to a specific set of concepts or ideas, and a terminology appropriate to the subject. There is also usually a history of debate of some kind that is important to the nature of the discourse.

Discourses may intersect with one another, or one may include, or be related to, another (or several others). Thus, the general discourse of literary theory includes discourse on ways of reading, as well as on the value and function of literature. It also includes the discourse of poetic theory, which in turn includes discourse oriented specifically towards ways of reading poems. These several discourses coincide with discourses on language, history, culture, and so on.

To enter a discourse, therefore, is to enter a dynamic of discussion, in which hypotheses are continually being made, or drawn from other discourses, and are then made part of an ongoing debate. Each time we read a poem, we enter into this discourse, whether we are aware of it or not. This is because the implicit or explicit theory (or theories) by which we read the text inevitably place us somewhere in the debate. By becoming aware of theory in general, and of particular theories, we can participate in this often exciting, and always stimulating debate. By contributing to it, we can come to an understanding of the history of the discourse.

Criticism is best understood as the application of a theory to specific texts. In practice, the distinction between theory and criticism is not hard and fast: many theoretical essays include, by way of exemplification, instances of critical writing.

The discourse with which we will be chiefly concerned, that of theories of poetry, views poetry as made up of particular elements. In broad terms, these include: *the text itself* — the language that makes the poem on the page; *the real or imaginary events or circumstances* to which the poem refers, or which it describes; the *role of the poet*, both in *writing* the poem, and *in* the poem itself (is the poet the actual speaker of the text?); the *role of the reader*; and *historical and cultural influences* on the possible meaning. The various theories we will examine address these elements in different ways, foregrounding some and backgrounding others. The poetic text can thus be made to produce a variety of readings or meanings.

What Theory or Theories Should We Adopt?

In the chapters that follow, we will investigate and outline several current theories. We will also consider the respective strengths and weaknesses of each. Further, we will trace the inter-relationships among them, in order to construct a sense of the historical dimensions of this particular discourse. In addition, we will see how a particular theory works in criticism of specific poetic texts.

New Criticism has been chosen as the starting point for several reasons. In the first place, for some sixty years, it has been a powerful influence in both literary criticism and the academic teaching of literature. Though not currently fashionable in contemporary critical circles, its doctrines and methodology are still being taught. As a still-functioning, though perhaps no longer central theory of literature and method of criticism, then, it cannot be neglected or ignored.

In the second place, as we shall see in the following chapter, New Criticism marked a break with older theories of literature that stressed a subjective response on the part of the reader and encouraged a kind of élitism in criticism. Inevitably, of course, New Criticism created its own élite, something that is eventually true of all kinds of theory. In the place of older sorts of criticism, New Criticism installed a theory that insisted on the importance of the text and of its patterning, both verbal and conceptual. In this, New Criticism reflects the contemporary interest in (some would say, obsession with) language and its processes.

It is important to realise that, though we will refer to the theories considered in this book as individual entities such as New Criticism, structuralism and so on, no theory is monolithic. We can find considerable variation in theory and practice among the different critics whom we label New Critics or structuralists, and so forth. Not only do they differ among themselves, but many of them move from one critical position to another in the course of their careers. This occurs for a number of reasons. The first, and most evident one, is simply the evolution of the theory in question. As its inadequacies or incompleteness are uncovered, it is further elaborated to deal with these.

Another reason is historical. A theory which emerges as a reaction against, or a contradiction of, another is likely to make its claims less subtly and more intransigently than a more established system of thinking. New Criticism is a case in point. Its early proponents made large claims for it (by which we should not, however, understand that their actual practices of reading were therefore simplistic). These became modified and more subtle as time went on and the theory became more widely accepted, and no longer had to fight for survival.

It is currently common practice among critics and historians of literary theory to insist on the *differences* between different theories, and to minimise the often considerable and important *continuities* from one theory to another. In this book, we will be looking more at such continuities, as a way to open inquiry into the discourse of literary theory. Such inquiry can only take place if we accept that there *is* a discourse, that is, a framework of ideas and concerns that the different theories share.

It should be evident by now that we, as readers, have already adopted at least one theory, though this may be implicit: we read in particular ways, and for particular reasons. Our question should perhaps therefore be rephrased: 'What *other* theory or theories should we adopt?'

Delightful and simple though it might be to be able to say, 'This one, but not that or that other', the answer to this question is not a simple one. At one level, we should recognise that if our present way of reading is suited to our purposes, there is no strong reason to adopt another theory and its method of reading. However, we rarely read all texts the same way. Moreover, as we develop our skills and scholarship in particular directions, some theories and their practices become more appropriate than others. Thus, it is important for us to have several theoretical strings to our bows, to enable us to handle different kinds of texts effectively, and at different points in our careers as students or scholars of literature.

We do not always read texts for the same reasons. We might engage with one poem in order to find out how it works; with another to see how it fits into the general scheme of its author's development as a poet; with a third to see how the poet's ideas or imagery evolved; and with a fourth in order to learn or confirm something about the culture or the period during which the text was written. All of these are valid reasons to read a poem, but no single method of reading will satisfy all intents equally.

It is, perhaps, misleading to talk about adopting different theories, as though they were homeless waifs. It is more useful to think of it as familiarising oneself with a range of them, not all of which will necessarily be applied in practical terms, but whose value often lies in allowing comparisons. In the same way, we don't usually buy important commodities — say, a car — without first seeing what products are on the market, comparing prices, examining differing features, what deals the company is willing to make, and so on. The same should be true of a literary theory. Any single theory will be able to do some things, but not others, and thus will provide certain advantages, not all of which relate purely to the reading of literary texts. For example, there may be status gained by belonging to a currently fashionable theoretical set. But to know exactly what a theory, like a car, can offer, we must know the capabilities of the other makes in the range.

When we become interested in theory, we might wish also to set about examining and comparing the various theories, to see where they achieve similar ends and where they differ, and for what reasons. This is likely to lead us to an investigation of the relation of particular theories to the kind of literature being written, and to cultural and historical influences that might have affected both the writing and the theorising. Thus, learning about theory can open doors on to other, often apparently unrelated areas, which can teach us a good deal about our culture, both past and present.

Another reason to learn about a variety of theories is as a means to evaluate the claims of particular theorists and their adherents. It has become popular, in the presence of so many different theories about literature, to cry up one's own particular brand at the expense of others. Thus the proponents of one approach are likely to make claims that their own theory is entirely new, when a careful study of other theories might reveal that its novelties are in fact merely restatements of ideas already available elsewhere. Alternatively, a theory may be set up as old-fashioned, partial, or in some other way in-adequate, where careful examination might show that it is being misrepresented. In other words, familiarity with a range of literary theories can act as a corrective measure against poor scholarship.

There is, however, a word of caution necessary here. Knowing many theories can easily lead to eclecticism of practice. In general, it is desirable that we be consistent in our approach to literary texts. This does not mean that the same theory and practice should be used forever, but that when we adopt a particular theory (and its practice), we understand why it is appropriate to a particular text and accept its limitations.

It also implies that where more than one practice is employed, these should not be philosophically or methodologically incompatible. Eclecticism invites us merely to become adept at using different practices of reading without reference to a particular theory, and can leave us open to accusations of lack of scholarship, of faddism, opportunism or expedience. Such practice creates a vacuum, since our method does not pay serious attention to the theories that inform specific practices of reading.

Selecting Key Theories

Though literary theory is the focus of this book, it is not intended that the book replace any of the more detailed, specialist discussions of contemporary literary theory that are currently widely available. The present work does not cover all current literary theory in an exhaustive manner. Rather, the book addresses the relevance of a selection of contemporary theories to the reading of poetic texts, and thus is designed to complement more detailed considerations.

To help you in your browsings through current theory, you should consult the Suggestions for Further Reading included at the end of each chapter. In this chapter, these direct you to general considerations of theory, and to several collections of primary theoretical essays. It is not always easy to distinguish between primary and secondary works about theory. Often, an essay on theory or applying a theory will itself be presenting and working through certain theoretical issues. The distinction between primary and secondary entries in the Suggestions, therefore, should be understood as somewhat arbitrarily drawn. In two subsequent chapters, Poetry and History and Poetry and Gender, the Suggestions are divided according to types of theory, rather than between primary and secondary categories. In later Suggestions, the abbreviated entries refer to works referenced fully at the end of the chapter.

The following chapters offer the appropriate *model* for each of the theories discussed, focusing on how each theory conceives of the nature of literature and criticism. At the same time, your attention is drawn to key images or terms typical of the theory. Further, the model is *contextualised*. The historical circumstances, including any relevant discussion of literary theories related or opposed to the one under consideration, are presented in brief form, in order to see how the relevant theory emerged, and why. Continuities between, and relationships among, different theories are pointed out.

In addition, some important *names* among the theorists and the titles of a few of their key works are given. These, however, are kept to a minimum, since it is the purpose of this book to show how the theories work in practice, rather than to set out each theory in all its detail. You are advised, therefore, to read the primary works yourself, and perhaps to follow up this reading by a look at some of the surveys listed at the end of this chapter.

Finally, we will consider the advantages and disadvantages of each theory, in terms of what it can and cannot do in practical application. Here, again, you may be referred to theories discussed in other chapters, to see how they may deal with particular problems, or how they may supplement the theory under discussion.

Notes

1. *Semiotics of Poetry*. London: Methuen, 1978: 1. References to works included in the Suggestions for Further Reading at the end of each chapter are given parenthetically in the text. Other occasional citations are endnoted.

Suggestions for Further Reading

Primary

Calderwood, James L., and Harold E. Toliver, eds. *Perspectives on Poetry*. New York: Oxford University Press, 1968.

Lodge, David, ed. *Modern Criticism and Theory: A Reader*. London and New York: Longman, 1988.

— ed. *20th Century Literary Criticism: A Reader*. London: Longman, 1972.

Perry, John Oliver, ed. *Approaches to the Poem: Modern Essays in the Analysis and Interpretation of Poetry*. San Francisco: Chandler, 1965.

Rice, Philip, and Patricia Waugh, eds. *Modern Literary Theory: A Reader*. London: Edward Arnold, 1989.

Rylance, Rick, ed. *Debating Texts: A Reader in Twentieth Century Literary Theory and Method*. Milton Keynes: Open University Press, 1987.

Secondary

Belsey, Catherine. *Critical Practice*. London and New York: Methuen, 1980.

Eagleton, Terry. *Literary Theory: An Introduction*. Oxford: Blackwell, 1983.

Hawthorn, Jeremy, ed. *Criticism and Critical Theory*. London: Edward Arnold, 1984.

Hošek, Chaviva, and Patricia Parker, eds. *Lyric Poetry: Beyond New Criticism*. Ithaca and London: Cornell University Press, 1985.

Jefferson, Ann, and David Robey, eds. *Modern Literary Theory: A Comparative Introduction*. London: Batsford, 1982.

Lentricchia, Frank. *After the New Criticism*. London: Methuen, 1983.

Machin, Richard, and Christopher Norris, eds. *Post-Structuralist Readings of English Poetry*. Cambridge: Cambridge University Press, 1987.

Selden, Raman. *A Reader's Guide to Contemporary Literary Theory*. Brighton: Harvester, 1985.

Sturrock, John, ed. *Structuralism and Since: From Lévi-Strauss to Derrida*. Oxford: Oxford University Press, 1979.

Wellek, René, and Austin Warren. *Theory of Literature*. 3rd edn. Harmondsworth: Penguin, 1963.

Young, Robert, ed. *Untying the Text: A Post-Structuralist Reader*. Boston: Routledge & Kegan Paul, 1981.

2
New Criticism

The term New Criticism came to be applied to a particular group of critics and theorists in the 1920s and 1930s after the publication of John Crowe Ransom's book, *The New Criticism*. As a theory of the literary text and how to read it, New Criticism has attracted unfavourable judgements throughout its existence. Ironically, some of these have come, in recent years, to echo the charges that were laid against the theory in its earlier formulations. For example, the New Critical attack on certain practices of reading was deemed to be grounded in a vain attempt to make literary study more 'scientific'. Today, however, New Criticism is often faulted for not being scientific enough.

It is, of course, easy to point out, with the advantage of hindsight, the self-contradictions and shortcomings of New Criticism. But it is important to familiarise ourselves with the historical circumstances that contributed to its rise, and which on occasion caused its proponents to maintain extreme positions which today may seem indefensible. In any case, most of the theorists (as is the case with the proponents of most theories) changed their positions gradually as circumstances changed, and New Criticism came to be accepted as a valid, useful theory of literature and of reading.

New Criticism originated in a response to three reading practices inherited from the nineteenth century, namely, belle-lettrism, impressionism,[1] and historicism. Belle-lettrism owes its name to the French term *belles-lettres*, meaning, literally, fine writing. Deriving from the nineteenth century admiration of Romantic attitudes and writing, and from the aestheticist codes which developed towards the end of that century, belle-lettrism refers to both the production and consumption of polite, elegant literature, and, in the nineteenth century, further signified the wider study of literature. The Romantics had characterised the writer as a person not only of special talent, but also of special sensibilities — a belief still current in our own culture. The ideal reader of such an author's work, according to belle-lettrist canons, was, therefore, someone with reciprocal sensibilities.

Aestheticism developed in the later part of the nineteenth century as an extreme (some might say decadent) form of Romanticism. This theory, rebelling against the developing materialism and pragmatism of the nineteenth century, argued that art served no ends but its own: art for art's sake. Indeed, this phrase may be attributed to Walter Pater,[2] one of the more influential voices in the belle-lettristic/ aestheticist theorising of art and literature. Certain formulations of his became catchwords and mottoes for a group of writers and readers. For example, Pater's dictum that *'All art constantly aspires toward the condition of music'* ('The School of Giorgione' 95; Pater's italics) means that art tends towards obliterating the distinction between content and form, and that this is most apparently achieved in music.

It was Pater, too, who proclaimed the aesthetic experience of life to be the preferred objective:

> Every moment some form grows perfect in hand or face; some tone on the hills or the sea is choicer than the rest; some mood of passion or insight or intellectual excitement is irresistibly real and attractive to us, — for that moment only. Not the fruit of experience, but experience itself, is the end... To burn always with this hard, gemlike flame, to maintain this ecstasy, is success in life ('Conclusion' 157–8)

The privileging of art as both different and separate from other human and social activities set not only the artist apart from other beings in the culture, but also the reader who could truly appreciate the artist's work, and, through the work, the artist him or herself. Put more crudely, a banker might be able to *buy* art, but only those of appropriate sensitivity and ability were able to *understand* it. (It may be instructive at this point to recall the old joke about not knowing much about art, but knowing what one likes: from the aestheticist perspective, this is precisely the attitude of the materialist.)

Another source of the development of belle-lettrism was the attitude towards the teaching of English literature in the schools of the later nineteenth century. The dominant object of literary study was classics, Greek and Latin language and literature. The introduction of English literature into the curriculum was at first regarded as undesirable, and then as appropriate to students of a certain (inferior) intelligence and social standing. (It is a symptom of the culture at that time that this category of student included women, for it was still unusual for women to further their education at tertiary level.)

Understandably, a reaction occurred against this conservative and élitist attitude towards vernacular literature. This, combined with the popular mystique centred on the figure of the artist led, as we have seen, to a certain defiance of attitude which created its own élitism in the notion that one either knows how to read well, or one does not. If one does, then one 'naturally' appreciates the fine quality of literature, in the same way that a gourmet appreciates fine food. An education in the field of literature could only refine and direct already existing ability, it was felt, and that ability could not be brought into being where no potential existed.

The traditional classical education was thus challenged as the best or, indeed, the only way to develop such natural talents. The challenge gradually, however, deteriorated into impressionism, the second practice of reading which New Criticism combated. In an impressionistic reading of a text, the reader's emotional response takes precedence over actual understanding of textual details, and the response is regarded as of prime importance. Being able to say what the *meaning* of a text is becomes less important than the ability to claim that one responds to or 'feels' that text. Indeed, 'literary appreciation' became a euphemism for a process that used the literary text as a way to induce an emotional response that did not always bear a strong relation to its meaning. Associations of a subjective kind took precedence over any objective meaning which the text might possess.

Historicist criticism was a product of nineteenth-century developments in history, archaeology and philology. As a way of reading literary texts, historicism sought to establish the historical context for the work, seek out the literary sources for and influences upon it, and situate it in the author's life. In other words, this practice transformed the literary work into an historical document: its chief value and practical meaning was its location in a certain epoch and in an author's life.

Thus the three practices of reading opposed by New Criticism were social (belle-lettrism), psycho-emotional and subjective (impressionism) and archival (historicism). None was oriented specifically towards the literary text itself. World War I, however, brought about many changes, both social and conceptual. These included attitudes towards the production and reception of literary texts. The old social order was demonstrated not only to be impermanent, but also fallible. Such undermining of apparently eternal truths and structures inherited from the preceding century opened up many areas of inquiry and judgement. The interrogation and subversion of an older order and its assumptions are exemplified in such movements in the world of art as Expressionism, Dada and Surrealism. These turned upside down traditional notions about how art represents reality, what appropriate subjects for art were, and how the viewer was to 'read' the work of art. In the world of literature, there also came a questioning of the assumptions of the older order concerning the special and privileged nature of the production and reception of literary texts, as well as a rejection of the cult of the personality in literature — the idea that only those with special abilities and sensitivity could write and read literature.

Two important points should be noted with reference to the origins and development of New Criticism. First, as I remarked in the first chapter, despite the practice of speaking of the New Critics as a single group, they by no means offered a single, unified theory, even though they shared a number of principles and assumptions.

We can divide the New Critics into several groups. One of these developed its approach to literature in England, where it came to be called 'practical criticism', and was associated with, among others, I.A. Richards, whose theory was chiefly linguistic. In discussing the function of literature, he adopted the approach of examining the reader's psychological and neural response to the literary text as a way of harmonising intellect and feeling in the reader's apprehension of the text's meaning. In *Practical Criticism,* his 1929 study of how readers actually read poetry, Richards proposed the coexistence of four kinds of meaning: *sense* (the thing spoken about); *feeling* (the attitude of the speaker towards the thing spoken about); *tone* (the attitude of the speaker towards the listener); and *intention* (the effect the speaker desires to promote) (181–2). This four-part segmentation of meaning, possible in all human utterance, and hence also in poetic texts, became a key strategy in the practice of literary criticism and — significantly — the teaching of that practice in England.

Another influence in the field was T.S. Eliot, an American transplanted to England, who argued for the special status of the literary text and its language. He included in his theorising about literature an emphasis on the importance of literary history in the placing of individual texts, and the process of interpreting them.

Associated with the British school of New Criticism was F.R. Leavis, who, together with his wife Q.D. Leavis, established a centre of theory and criticism at Cambridge University. The Leavises also founded the quarterly journal *Scrutiny,* whose first issue appeared in May 1932. This journal reached a wider community of both general readers and academic scholars, and disseminated the pugnacious, adversarial ideas of the Leavises and their group.[3] Dismissing as effete and bloodless the Edwardian literature admired by the self-professed intellectual élite and academics, the Leavisites attacked what they called 'the reach and thoroughness of the Literary Racket, and the power and vindictiveness of the gangs' (F.R. Leavis, 'The Literary Racket', *Scrutiny* 1: 160). By 'gangs' was intended the apparatus by which the literary status quo was maintained. This included the old boys' network of individuals who had been to school and to university together; the scholars whose concern was with establishing an editorially proper text, and not with what that text might mean; and the literary reviewers who seemed to belong to a club designed to protect certain literary interests and tastes. In place of this 'Literary Racket', the Leavisites wished to establish a literary criticism that would be intellectually more open and honest, and a literary canon, dubbed, in the words of the title of one of F.R. Leavis' books, 'The Great Tradition'. The characteristics of this tradition were moral as much as literary, in that authenticity and sincerity of feeling, for instance, were deemed valuable in a work of literature.[4]

William Empson's *Seven Types of Ambiguity* also proved an important theoretical text in New Criticism in England. In this work, Empson, a student of Richards, explores the ways in which the language of a literary text opens out onto complexities of meaning deriving from the etymology of the words themselves, from their cultural associations, and from the pressures of the context in which they are located. Empson's methodology coincides with that of the American New Critics, on some of whose work it was a critical influence.

One group of these consisted principally of practising poets, some of whom evolved their theories outside the academic establishment, and were profoundly influenced by Eliot, among others. They included Allen Tate, John Crowe Ransom and Cleanth Brooks. Another group was located within academia, and developed the New Critical theory along more scholarly and traditional lines. Among these may be included theorists like R.S. Crane and Elder Olson, members of the so-called Chicago School based at the University of Chicago. There, interest in Aristotle's analytic methods resulted, in the field of literary theory, in particular attention to the formal aspects of the literary text. (However, we should note that the Chicago critics did not consider themselves to be New Critics, and indeed often attacked New Criticism for the lack of system in its theory. Likewise, F.R. Leavis and William Empson are generally included in the English New Critical school, though they, too, often had differences with many New Critical assumptions and practices.)

The second important point to bear in mind is that though the New Criticism emerged as a revolution against older schools of criticism, its theories were inevitably influenced by those schools. For example, the theory of literary organicism, which underpins much New Critical theorising about literature, is to be found elaborated in the work of Coleridge, yet many of the New Critics railed against the Romantics as Establishment poets, and protested against their influence, especially in the universities, where Romantic poetry and theory held sway.

The influence of Romanticism is to be seen in the way New Criticism both conceives of literature and invents terms by which to discuss it. The theory of organic form put forward by the Romantic poet-critics, especially Coleridge, is founded on the assumption that the poem:[5]

> begins as a 'seed' or 'germ' in the creative imagination of the poet; its growth, primarily an unconscious process, consists in assimilating to itself foreign and diverse materials; its development and final form are self-determined; the result is like a living thing in that multiplicity and unity, the particular and the universal, content and form have coalesced and fused.

The adoption of this notion had several important consequences for New Critical theory.

In the first place, it permitted the New Critics to argue that if the poetic text imitates or participates in natural processes, and is produced out of these, its meaning must be accessible to all readers, since they also share in these natural processes. In this way, New Criticism opened up the meaning-making process in literature to everyone. In practice, however, the theory shifts the focus of the argument about accessibility from the natural abilities of the reader to the naturalness of the methods of the theory, in which the reader can be easily trained. This in no way implies that New Criticism is therefore a simplistic, or even a simple, theory. The rhetoric of the practical demonstrations of New Criticism at work, however, strongly suggests that, given the proper instruction, any reader can easily make similar sense of a literary text. This is one of the reasons New Criticism gained a strong foothold in academic institutions in most places in the English-speaking world: its rhetorical (though often only implicit) claim to make the literary text available was accessible in its apparent democracy to both teachers and students.

The principle of organic form offered another attraction. If the literary text *is* organic in that its parts all work together to create a harmonious whole that mirrors nature, the text, it can be argued, is a self-sufficient entity, just as plants and animals are. Questions about the historical circumstances surrounding the gestation and completion of the text become largely irrelevant, except perhaps as ways of establishing a sort of genus-species identity, or a pedigree for the text, or to explain certain features of it, such as peculiarities of diction or grammar, much as the peculiarities of a prize dog or cat can be explained by the animal's ancestry. What is important is the text's presence on the page. This alone allows it to be understood and responded to without reference to information and detail that are largely external. Thus, New Critics developed the Romantic idea of organicism in a particular direction. By shifting the emphasis from the poet's organising consciousness to the verbal structure of the text itself, they were able to view it as at least partially independent of the historical circumstances and context surrounding its creation.

Meaning in a text thus becomes heavily dependent upon the analysis of its form. Just as a plant doesn't have a 'meaning' outside the matter of which it is composed and the structure by which that matter is organised, so a poem's meaning is to be derived from a close examination of the matter — the words — of which it is made, and the structure — the grammar, syntax and rhetoric, as well as various formal patterns — in which that matter is arranged. Content — that is, meaning — thus becomes inseparable from form: you cannot carry away the meaning of the poem as though it were some precious fluid poured out of a useful and attractively decorated, but otherwise unimportant, container. The container must also be accounted for.

The tying together of form and content disposed in an elegant way of the hitherto accepted literary-critical tradition, derived from the preference for forensic (that is, persuasive) classical rhetoric: that figurative language in poetry is mere decoration. If form and content are inseparable, the way in which a poet chooses to express him or herself has a direct bearing on the meaning. To express the idea any other way would be in fact *to change that idea substantially*. Figurative language thus becomes more than mere embellishment of an idea, and able to be separated from the words expressing it: figures such as metaphor actually affect the meaning of the text.

For this reason, the New Critics warned against what they called the heresy of paraphrase (see Brooks, *The Well Wrought Urn* 192–214). The paraphrase of a poetic text can be undertaken solely on the assumptions not only that the meaning or idea or 'message' of the text is separable from its expression, but also that the relation of form to content is unproblematic.

This is connected also to the principle of organic form as a defining feature of literary texts. Just as, in nature, a tree is itself, and no other thing, or a dog is itself, and not a cat, so also a poem is self-identifying and autonomous. In order to argue this, the New Critics postulated that the language of which poetry is made differs in several important ways from the language of everyday speech and of other kinds of non-literary texts.

When we deal with non-literary, especially non-poetic, texts, we tend to assume that their language operates like a pane of clear glass, giving us access to the meaning of the utterance or piece of writing. Moreover, we also suppose that this meaning refers us to things, persons or events in the real world. Thus, a statement such as 'It is raining heavily all over the region' may be taken as a straightforward meteorological description of a real event.

However, language in literary texts has a double function. One of its operations is, of course, to provide a denotative meaning referring to objects, events and people, whether real or imaginary. Its more important task in literature, however, is to emphasise the linguistic features of the text, and to heighten and intensify their effect on the denotative meaning. This is achieved by the use of many devices: for example, unusual diction; a strong reliance on figurative language such as metaphor and symbol; the introduction of highly suggestive and connotative words and images which invest the literal, denotative meanings with a shadowing of other possible significations; and striking patterns and structures of words and sounds, as well as the syntactical or rhetorical arrangements of these, together with the similar patterning of images. In other words, the verbal structure of the literary text is highly wrought. Thus, though we might treat the language of non-literary texts as though it were transparent, we find that literary language, by contrast, demands attention, because it is often opaque, difficult, and in need of close examination.

The effect of this careful and intensified use of language in poetic texts is to create a verbal context within the text against which individual effects are to be measured. The pressure of this context against the text's individual features not only helps define the meaning of these features, but also brings about the presence in the text of *irony*. A particular use of this term in New Critical theory means an awareness of contradictions, ambiguities or paradoxes (often merely latent in the meanings of the words themselves) which extend the possibilities of meaning in the text. Thus, in our example above, the statement 'It is raining heavily all over the region' becomes more than a description of the weather if it is located in a poem dealing with the loss or death of love: it then becomes a metaphor which imposes the speaker's sorrow on his or her surroundings. If the line were to occur in a poem about war and its effects, its meaning would become correspondingly different. The *literal*, meteorological meaning is not lost, but the context created by the poem exerts a pressure on the line so that it means something altogether different from an observation about the rotten weather. This pressure is that of irony.

The assumption that the poetic text is self-enclosed and self-determining in meaning leads, in New Criticism, to a view of the text as an object. Though it is made up of words which constitute an essentially temporal medium (that is, whose meaning unfolds serially in time), the poem's structure invites us to consider it much as we would a statue or a painting: that is, to see it as a totality of meaning, rather than as a sequence of constituent words and sounds. To put it differently, we are asked to approach the poem as a sort of three-dimensional object existing in *space* rather than in time. The titles of a number of the key New Critical works indeed suggest this notion of the text as object: for example, *The Well Wrought Urn* (an urn is generally a decorated vase, often used simultaneously, literally or

symbolically, to hold the ashes of the dead and to provide an aestheti-
cally pleasing ornament), *The Verbal Icon* (an icon is a picture or a
painting, and often carries the implication of decoration), *The World's
Body* (here, the notion of organic form is fused with the idea of the
model from which art draws its inspiration).

Despite the desire of the New Critics to adopt the rigour of science
as an element of literary analysis, and despite their emphasis on the
need to pay close attention to the linguistic and verbal features of
literary texts, New Criticism failed to evolve or adopt any thorough-
going theory about language itself. This is something of a curiosity in
a literary theory which foregrounds the text's language so strongly,
particularly as developments were taking place in the fields of linguistics
and stylistics which could well have been borrowed for, or adapted to,
the purposes of New Criticism. A partial explanation for this neglect
may be found in the general rejection by the New Critics of science as
a mode of inquiry. Though they wished to objectify the study of
literature, and make it a scholarly discipline with the rigour of scientific
inquiry, rather than leave it as a field for gifted amateurs only, many
of these critics held science responsible for what T.S. Eliot called 'the
dissociation of sensibility' ('The Metaphysical Poets', *Selected Essays*
287–8), that is, the fragmentation of human consciousness so that
society could never again possess the unity and direction that it once
had. Eliot and others fixed on the late Renaissance as the period when
that unified sensibility reached its peak of achievement, before it
dissolved and disintegrated in the pursuit of science and technology.

For many of these critics, poetry represented a means whereby a
temporary unity could be achieved. The operation of irony in the
poetic text was regarded not as a device of fragmentation, but of
unification, whereby disparate and often conflicting elements could be
brought together, and, for the duration of the reader's experience of
the poem, placed in a harmonious relation with one another. In an
important way, therefore, literary language both reflected reality as a
series of discontinuous, contradictory and ambiguous experiences,
and showed a possible ideal reconciliation of those discontinuities by
means of a single, harmonious, literary experience.

For this to take place, several assumptions had to be made regarding
the text. The first was the independence of the text from its author.
Attention to the author of the text distracts from the centrality of the
text itself, and is more likely to emphasise the dissociation of sensibility than to harmonise disparity. For the awareness of an authorial
presence creates a gap between reader and text, highlights historical
differences, and tends to weight the text's meaning in favour of the
known or assumed intention of the author.

Therefore, New Criticism discourages investigation not only into
the biography and psychology of the author, but also into the author's

intention in writing the poem. In 'The Intentional Fallacy', an important essay written in collaboration with Monroe Beardsley, and included in *The Verbal Icon*, W.K. Wimsatt, Jr attacks the idea that the meaning of a poem depends on the author's intention when writing it. Wimsatt argues, among other things, that authorial intention is both notoriously unstable — authors have been known to change their minds in the midst of writing a work — and notoriously inaccessible, since in many cases, we have no way of finding out exactly the author's intentions (the case of Shakespeare, about whose private life and authorial intentions almost nothing is known, may serve as an illustration). In other words, the authors themselves either have not known their intentions, or have refused or been unable to make them public.

On the other hand, we do have the poem, which must embody a meaning of some kind, whether this falls within the author's intention or not. The 'author's meaning' is either there on the page, or it is forever obscured from us. No amount of biographical research should be allowed to deform the text and its meaning into a reading of authorial intent. If the author did his or her job properly, his or her intention is part of the meaning we make in the text; if he or she did not, then that intention is irrelevant to that meaning.

If neither the poet nor the poet's intention in writing the poem is central to the meaning of the text, then it makes little sense to talk of the poem as spoken by the poet. Therefore, the New Critics prefer to talk about the *speaking voice, addresser* or *persona* of the poem. The last term, a Latin word meaning 'mask', is suggestive: the poet, instead of speaking in his or her own guise, dons a personality by means of a set of verbal characteristics. These *may* coincide with those of the real poet: but it is not necessary to know whether they do or not in order to make sense of the text. Thus, though Robert Browning *may* be speaking in and for himself in his poem 'Home-Thoughts, From Abroad', in which the speaker, away from England, nostalgically thinks about spring in his home country, he clearly does not speak in his own voice in 'My Last Duchess': to assume that it *is* Browning who speaks in the latter poem would be to ignore the fact that the poet was a nineteenth-century Englishman who eloped with the woman he loved and who was to be his wife, and to put in his place the sinister and fantastic figure of the High Renaissance Duke of Ferrara, who, having had his previous duchess murdered, now negotiates for a new bride.

The substitution of a persona for the author allows the reader freer play in making sense of the text. We should not, however, assume therefore that the text can be made to mean whatever we want. The verbal structure, while it permits a number of possible readings, many of which may be layered over one another, is the final authority for meaning in the text. New Criticism assumes that the multiplicity of meaning is vested *in the text*, not in the reader — an important distinction, since structuralist and post-structuralist theory assumes the reverse.

The New Critical attitude towards the author implies another crucial issue: the attitude of this theory towards history. A common misapprehension of New Criticism is that it is entirely ahistorical. While it is true that the New Critics did not emphasise the role of history in their theory and practice, it is not true, as many detractors of the theory claim, that they abolished it altogether. First, the emphasis by Eliot and others on the importance of literary history itself implies a respect for historical concerns (see Eliot's 'Tradition and the Individual Talent', *Selected Essays* 13–22).

The New Critics were, moreover, aware of the historical dimension of language itself. They recognised that historical circumstances, including the linguistic, might well have produced a reading different from the one that a reader today might construct. Brooks in fact says this in his influential *Well Wrought Urn*:

> In order to understand Shakespeare, we simply have to understand what Shakespeare's words mean. And the implications of this latter point are immense: for they go far beyond the mere matter of restoring a few obsolete meanings. Tied in with language may be a way of apprehending reality, a philosophy, a whole worldview. And the last person who can afford to deny the importance of the shadings of language is the person like myself who attaches great importance to the connotations, the feeling tone, the nuances of the poet's words. The problem has to be faced, and it is not an easy one. (236)

This, argues Brooks, means that the reader must deal with poems of other times in the same way as with poems of other languages: in other words, the reader must accept a degree of 'translation' in order to make sense of the text.

The danger in the strongly historical approach for the New Critics, however, is that we might 'identify the "poetry" with certain doctrines or with certain emotional effects which automatically proceed from a certain historical conditioning' (236). For New Criticism, poetry remains poetry, and hence accessible to its reader, regardless of the historical conditions which contributed to its production. To tie meaning in a poem to those historical conditions is to accept historical relativism. In any case, since in general we are unable to know absolutely all the details pertaining to the historical circumstances surrounding the composition of a poem, much less perfectly recreate these, the New Critics felt that the historical argument in reading poetry was ultimately vain when it came to saying what the poem was *about*.[6]

It was for this reason that Archibald MacLeish's poem 'Ars Poetica', with its famous provocative lines, 'Poetry should not mean/ But be,' became something of a battle-standard for the New Critics. The poem asserts the integrity and evocativeness of poetic texts, defying the traditional forms of critical approach which anatomise such texts, relegating their various limbs and members to other, non-literary fields, such as history, biography, psychology and so forth. In this sense, a poem must not be made to 'mean', but should be approached as a phenomenal object, that is, an object-in-the-world.

If the author is absent from the text, and cannot determine its meaning, the reader's role is correspondingly made more important. However, what the New Critics desired to combat, as we have seen, was the impressionistic or subjective kind of reading that encourages the reader merely to 'respond to' or 'appreciate' the text, without being required to make *specific* as well as intelligible meaning of that text (see, for example, 'The Affective Fallacy' in *The Verbal Icon* 21–39).

To admit the reader as a determiner of textual meaning is to run the risk that a factor of instability will enter the process of making meaning. Different readers, in different circumstances, or even the same reader in different moods, will produce highly variable readings of a poem. These variations should not be allowed to become the meaning of the text, which, though multilevelled in its possible significations, is made up of a stable verbal structure, and ought to offer a meaning which is not dependent, however rich it may be, on the vagaries of the reader's state of mind or physical circumstances.

To guarantee the stability of the poetic text, New Criticism postulates two recipients of it. First, there is the *ostensible* or *apparent* recipient: the beloved to whom the text is addressed, the speaker's self, the nation, and so on: the possibilities are varied and infinite. In most cases, this ostensible addressee cannot be identified with the actual reader, otherwise we would all simper and blush as we read love poems, for instance.

The second recipient is an *idealised reader*, as opposed to the actual reader, and is created, like the ostensible addressee, by the text — the kind of language used, the grammatical structures and rhetorical strategies deployed, and so on. It is then up to the actual reader to try to accommodate him or herself to this idealised reader. The degree of 'fit' will affect the degree to which the text opens up to the actual reader, and will, moreover, determine the degree of subtlety of reading, as well as how 'acceptable' the poem might be. For example, a poem which requires us as actual readers to demonstrate specialised knowledge, or to approve of social or political attitudes or actions that are in fact objectionable to us will prove less open than other poems.

Thus, we, like the poet, must create a kind of persona which allows us, first, to receive the text as its intended recipient — the speaker's mistress, the speaker's self, and so on; and, second, to read that same text as its ideal reader. This strategy or procedure guarantees to a greater or lesser extent the further operation of the irony so valued by the New Critics, since the possible different meanings of the text for ostensible recipient, ideal reader and actual reader will tend to create the sort of dislocations of sense which allow of ironical readings. Any already existing dislocations of this kind, of course, will then be foregrounded and emphasised.

Thus, the poet creates the poem which generates the speaking identity or persona. This speaker appears to utter the text which is to be read. The actual reader produces two reading *personae*. One is that of the ideal reader, the one imagined by the poet as receiving the poetic text. This reader is aware of the structures and strategies operating in the text. The other reading persona is that of the apparent addressee of the utterance, the person to whom the speaker is talking, and who in general is more naïve and 'innocent' than the ideal reader persona. For this reading persona, the actual reader must imagine him or herself to be the speaker's interlocutor.

The assumption of the presence of a speaker and an addressee also includes the assumption of a particular dramatic situation: the persona speaks of and in a certain context, to a listener who is in some way relevant to that, if only as a confidant. This dramatic situation thus also presupposes *a social relationship* between speaker and listener — as equals, as superior and inferior (or vice versa), as lover and beloved, and so on. This social relationship, combined with the dramatic situation, generates the *tone* of the poem, which the reader reconstructs through the kind of language used in the text (see Brower 19–30).

It is likely that the fondness displayed by the New Critics for poetry from the late sixteenth and early seventeenth centuries is related to the New Critical idea of the dramatic situation created in the poetic text. This era saw the flourishing of the theatre in England and much of the poetry of the time displays certain theatrical features, such as, for instance, the stage monologue. However, this does not imply that New Criticism dealt exclusively with Renaissance poetry, although its practitioners were responsible for the elevation of poets like Donne and Marvell from the relative obscurity to which they had been consigned by the turn of the twentieth century. At the same time, the New Critics, because so many of them were practising poets as well as theorists, invited interest in contemporary poetry. Thus, in two ways these critics flew in the face of traditional academic literary study —

by foregrounding both Renaissance and twentieth-century poetry at a time when eighteenth-century, Romantic and Victorian poetry dominated the academic curriculum.

The reading process, then, is a strategy whereby the reader temporarily relinquishes his or her own identity in order to enter the world of the poem, and understand it, as it were, from within.[7] This is one way in which New Critical theory preserves the autonomy of the poetic text.

Though the New Critics were careful always to signal that their use of the term 'poetry' included all literature, in fact much of their important work neglected fictional and dramatic texts — excluding the verse dramas of the Renaissance. The principal reasons for this are first, that lyric poetry is typically easier to work with, because such poems are generally shorter than fictional and dramatic texts. This, then, is a reason of expedience: in wishing to demonstrate their theory in practice, the New Critics were concerned to provide examples that could be grasped easily and in whole form.

The second reason is that of clarity of method. The interpretation of poetic texts permits the clearer demonstration of formal structures operating in these, as well as the functioning of irony. However, the methods of New Critical theory may be applied with equal success to both fictional and dramatic works.

Finally, we should consider in which ways the essentially semiotic practices of New Criticism had what may be termed mimetic qualities. In the first place, though the New Critics did not develop a language theory, as already remarked, theirs was not, therefore, a naïve view of the nature and function of language, particularly with reference to how it works in literature. As their insistence on the constant relation of form to content indicates, the New Critics came close to the later structuralist position which maintains that language shapes reality. However, unlike the structuralists, the New Critics were not prepared to commit themselves to the idea that we are in fact trapped in language, and its arbitrary structures. They insisted on the existence of a reality external to language, a reality *to which language points*, and the perception of which may be *shaped* by language, but which is not, as structuralist theory maintains, actually *created* by language.

Thus, though the New Critics stressed and worked with rhetorical patterns in the poems they examined, they were far from assuming that the poems were simply exercises in rhetoric. Poetry reflects a reality outside itself, not in the easy and reductive sense of being a transliteration of real events or people, but in the larger, more philosophical sense of alluding to human relationships, or historical situations in a manner that seems convincing and true, even though these events, people and situations may have been only fictional.

If poetry can reflect the world in this manner, it can also change that world by working on the reader's sensibilities and awareness. Put differently, we can learn about ourselves and the society and world we inhabit through the careful interpretation of poetry, and this education can enable us to change our environments and our social relationships for the better. Brooks remarks that 'One of the "uses" of poetry, I should agree, is to make us better citizens' ('Irony as a Principle of Structure' 211). Poetry, therefore, enjoys a double relationship with reality, according to New Criticism. On the one hand, poetry is passive: it mirrors both the structures and the disparities of reality. On the other, it is active: it reacts upon reality: 'Finding its proper symbol, defined and refined by the participating metaphors, the theme [of the poem] becomes a part of the reality in which we live — an insight, rooted in and growing out of concrete experience, many-sided, three-dimensional' (Brooks 211: note, incidentally, the reference to organicism, and implicitly also to the poem as 'three-dimensional' object in this observation). Seen in this way, poetry is a powerful and important mechanism in human social structures. Small wonder, therefore, that the New Critics were so loud and urgent in their appeals to their readers to learn how to read texts well.

New Criticism in Practice

Let us see how the theory works in practice by looking at Shakespeare's Sonnet 73:

> That time of year thou mayst in me behold
> When yellow leaves, or none, or few, do hang
> Upon those boughs which shake against the cold,
> Bare ruined choirs, where late the sweet birds sang.
> In me thou see'st the twilight of such day
> As after sunset fadeth in the west;
> Which by and by black night doth take away,
> Death's second self, that seals up all in rest.
> In me thou see'st the glowing of such fire,
> That on the ashes of his youth doth lie,
> As the deathbed whereon it must expire,
> Consumed with that which it was nourished by.
> This thou perceiv'st, which makes thy love more strong,
> To love that well which thou must leave ere long.

The structure of this sonnet follows a pattern typical of Shakespeare's sonnets in general. There are three quatrains, followed by a couplet, a structure cutting across that of the Italian model, which consists of an octave (eight lines) followed by a sestet (six lines). The opening quatrain typically establishes a situation, a mood, a problem or issue, and even an image cluster, which the succeeding two quatrains render more specific, develop and vary. The concluding couplet resolves the theme begun in the first quatrain, its expression suggesting an undeniable truth. Traces of the originating Italian model of the sonnet are still to be found in the ninth line (the beginning of the sestet), where the *volta* or 'turn' focuses the sonnet's theme more sharply, and introduces some interesting, even surprising, development.

A careful reading of the text, attention being paid not only to the denotations but also to the metaphoric and connotative meanings of the words, shows that the poem may be read on three levels. The first initiates and develops the theme of the speaker's sense of fleeting time and of his own decay through age. The second relates this thematic preoccupation to a consideration and rejection of traditional Christian responses to death, and encompasses briefly the historical issue of the Reformation in England. The third level of meaning addresses a theme that runs throughout Shakespeare's sonnets, namely, the concern with art (and with poetry in particular), and its ability to commemorate humanity and to outlive those who inspired it.

However, it is important to note that all three levels of meaning in this poem are related to one another. The first level establishes a theme or direction for the sonnet which governs the other two. Connotation is neither random nor subjective in a New Critical reading: all connotative meanings of the words employed in the text must contribute to the general sense and structure initiated at the first level of meaning, or else they remain marginal to the text's meaning.

The three quatrains, at the first level of meaning, develop two ideas which are metaphorically related to one another. One is that of time, envisaged at first as a seasonal or cyclical occurrence, and shown as continually narrowing in scope. In the first quatrain, this notion is imaged as the season in which 'yellow leaves, or none, or few, do hang/ Upon those boughs which shake against the cold,' suggesting late autumn or early winter. In the second quatrain, the image of time takes form as the twilight moment between day and night — 'the twilight of such day/ As fadeth in the west.' We have thus moved from an annual temporal cycle to a diurnal one; and in the third quatrain, even this is narrowed to 'the glowing of such fire,/ That on the ashes of his youth doth lie.' In this further limiting of the temporal moment, the sonnet shifts from an event which repeats itself according to the seasons of the year or of the day, to an event which is unique and which will be irretrievably lost when concluded. At first sight, these three temporal images appear to be alternatives intended to express with increasing force the notion of the end of a sequence. However, first, the narrowing of the idea of time itself and, second, the transformation of the repetitious into the unique, indicate that another theme is being developed at the same time.

The second idea developed through this sequence of images is that of human age and, specifically, the speaker's sense of his own decline. It is in him that the addressee may perceive signs of autumn, of coming night and of extinction. These are traditional metaphors, of course, but in this context, in connection with the shift which we have noted in the imagery of time, the metaphors are reworked to focus the addressee's (and the reader's) attention on the singularity of the speaker's life against the other changes occurring in nature. Read in this way, the quatrains suggest that though it is a part of life to age and die, it is nonetheless a matter of great import to the individual, whose physical decay and death occur against the universal cycles of growth, decay and rebirth.

This is signalled by the reiterated first person pronoun, which occurs at the beginning of each quatrain in an accented position in the line: 'That time of year thou mayst in *me* behold ...,' 'In *me* thou see'st the twilight of such day ...,' 'In *me* thou see'st the glowing of such fire ...' The couplet, however, emphasises the seer, not the object seen: 'This *thou* perceiv'st ...' The addressee is thus led through the series of metaphors from a commonplace about human life (that is, that it can be likened to the natural seasons) to a protest *against* such a complacent and unsympathetic cliché. The speaker demands, through the repeated use of verbs of sight, that his listener *see* him as an individual close to death, and not simply as the illustration of a standard truism about the brevity of human existence.

We may say that this level of meaning is addressed to the apparent recipient of the utterance embodied by the poem. The speaker is concerned not only to lament his own approaching end, but to elicit sympathy and affection from his listener, and to attribute to that listener an increase in love caused precisely by sympathy.

At the same time, on the second level of meaning, the metaphors operating in the quatrains develop further meanings which both reinforce the central meaning in the sonnet, and provide an ironic commentary upon it. It is at this point that the text's meaning is addressed, not to an ostensible listener, but to an ideal reader sensitive to changes in tone and to subtleties of meaning.

In the first quatrain, the palsy of old age is metaphorised in the shaking of the boughs of a tree in the cold. The quatrain concludes with an image that is retrospective in nature: 'Bare ruined choirs where late the sweet birds sang.' At one stroke, the introduction of the idea of 'choirs' transforms the trees of the earlier image into the skeletal remains of a mediaeval church, whose architecture included the choirstalls as a feature, and reminds us of the church as a place of worship.[8] The sense of nostalgia, extending from the idea of the ruined church to the memory of the birds which sang in the branches, reminding the speaker in turn of ecclesiastical architecture, also suggests a sense of deep and permanent loss.

The Church, as an institution, advises humanity to find consolation in the fact that mortality is a universal affliction, and is, moreover, humanity's own fault, through the original sin of Adam. In the present state of mind of the speaker, this is bankrupt counsel. Its bankruptcy is signalled by the decrepitude of the physical church constructed in this quatrain. The image of a ruined church would have had immediate signficance, both as a physical fact and as a metaphysical concept, to Shakespeare's contemporaries, who still had to deal with the consequences of Henry VIII's establishment of the Protestant faith in England, together with the seizure of Church properties. For many, this religious revolution caused much moral pain and posed many ethical problems. The dismantling in England of mediaeval Catholicism must have meant the disappearance of certain unquestioned values which, regardless of their ultimate theological status, provided a comforting and familiar view of humankind in both the physical and metaphysical universes.

In the second quatrain, the image of the day's end merges into another image, that of night, which the speaker declares to be 'Death's second self, that seals up all in rest.' Since Renaissance texts tend generally to speak of *sleep*, rather than night, as death's second self, this constitutes a curious transfer of meaning which makes of the absence of light itself a figure of death. The darkness of night thus has two meanings, in the context of this poem: in one meaning, it promises sleep, and, implicitly, awakening — it 'seals up in rest' — at both the level of the daily cycle of existence, and that of the cycle of human life. However, this is a doctrine generated by religious theory, by the very institution which, in the earlier quatrain, has been shown to be emptied of value.

The second meaning of 'night', therefore, denies the consolation of life eternal. The sealing up in rest is a permanent one, as one seals a body in a tomb. Night is now not merely an analogue of death as sleep is, according to mediaeval and Renaissance theology and philosophy: 'Death's *second* self', it is also death's double: 'Death's second *self*', and represents the truth of the grave. The sense of loss present in the first quatrain is here extended, and developed further.

The third quatrain also uses a metaphor common in Renaissance literature. The image of the fire that consumes its youth is an elaboration of the idea of the phoenix, the fabulous Arabian bird which, at the term of its life, builds its own funeral pyre and bursts spontaneously into flame. Out of this self-immolation comes the egg which, hatching in the warmth of the ashes, produces the new phoenix. The phoenix is thus unique, since it is self-generating; it needs no mate and produces no young. The image of fire, when associated with the phoenix, indicates rebirth: youth consumes old age eternally, and thus the creature lives forever. The image of the phoenix, moreover, was used as a symbol of the risen Christ in late mediaeval and Renaissance iconography. Jesus thus becomes the human equivalent of the creature which renews itself eternally.

However, in Shakespeare's poem, the speaker sees himself as a phoenix which will not regenerate itself. The uniqueness of the mythical bird is here wedded to the idea of the unique individual life which we have already noted in the first level of meaning of the sonnet. The notion that individuals are unique stems ultimately from the fact that we are mortal: however, where the doctrines of Christianity assert eternal life after death, the speaker of this poem stresses the finality of death. This phoenix will not rise from its ashes, and its failure to do so ironically guarantees its uniqueness.

In the concluding couplet, the speaker observes that his addressee's love corresponds in intensity to the awareness of the finality of the speaker's death. The phrasing in this couplet suggests strongly that the speaker sees himself as reaching a point of motionlessness in the movement of life which will carry his addressee farther on: the beloved loves 'that well which *thou must leave* ere long'. The temporal movement of the quatrains — the seasonal cycle, the diurnal cycle, the evolution of the fire towards its own extinction — is arrested at the end of the sonnet with this image of the immobility of death as against the movement of life. Thus, both levels of meaning which we have been considering conclude with a rejection of any notion of life after death.[9]

The remaining level of meaning, however, does offer a particular version of eternal life: the immortality to be achieved through art. The first quatrain introduces this theme in its image of the 'Bare ruined choirs, where late the sweet birds sang.' The idea of singing, here incorporated into the architectural image of a choir, and reinforced by the image of the birds which used to sing in the once-splendid trees, is a common metaphor for poetry. The total metaphor of the opening quatrain thus suggests not only the physical decay of the speaker, imaged as part of a natural cycle, but also his sense of his own decline as a poet.

Another image commonly used of the poet is that of the dreamer, of the person inspired by visions. However, in the second quatrain, the idea of sleep, typically associated with dreams and visions, is negated by its association with death. The sonnet has, through the previous levels which we have discussed, moved towards the notion that the sleep of death is dreamless. The poet who succumbs to this sleep will not write of the visions he sees.

The second quatrain also introduces the idea of light in 'the twilight of such day'. Illumination and fire have traditionally been images associated with poetry. The former refers to the truth which poetry is supposed to transmit, while the latter refers to the inspiration which motivates poetry. The third quatrain, accordingly, focuses on the image of fire, and again evokes the image of the spent poet confronted with the fact of his extinction, not only as a man, but as a poet. His past achievements ('the ashes of his youth') constitute the foundation ('the deathbed') of his now failing poetic power, which is 'Consumed with that which it was nourished by'.

If the sonnet is read in this fashion, the couplet suggests that the addressee may be seen as the source and object of the poet's inspiration. As such, the addressee must move on, though feeling strong affection for the speaker, to inspire other, more potent poets. This, after all, is the nature of inspiration.

Each of the quatrains presents a moment of transition between states of existence. In the first, the confusion created by the description that 'yellow leaves, or none, or few' hang on the speaker's metaphorical boughs suggests a seasonal transition between autumn (when yellow leaves are in abundance) and winter (when none are to be seen). In the second quatrain, the transitional moment is twilight, that moment between day and night, while in the third quatrain the transition is that instant of suddenly radiated light and warmth which occurs after the fire begins to die, but before total extinction takes place. However, whereas the quatrains all describe the speaker in this marginal state of being, the couplet places the addressee in a similar position: the addressee's love, says the speaker, is intensified by the addressee's awareness that the object of that love will shortly be gone.

The emphasis on transition between states of being, rather than on those states themselves, suggests the sense on the speaker's part that we are always *between* states of existence, or, at another level, between moments of historical significance. That sense of constant unease adds greatly to the pathos of the poem, at the first level: the speaker laments his own decay, which we may see as a model for our own. We are continually between the beginning of life and its end, and in that sense humanity as a whole lives in a transitional condition of being.

This bleak truth is, in the poem, rendered even more unpalatable by the exclusion of orthodox religious doctrine as consolation to us, who are always about to die. The promise of life after death is shown as illusory in the presence of death itself. Only art escapes death, and here the sonnet suggests that this is small comfort to the artist, whose powers must undergo the process of decline until their termination with the end of the artist's life itself. In sum, the sonnet voices the common cry of humanity when it is forced not only to undergo the decay both of physical existence and of intellectual powers, but also to accept the consciousness of that decay.

This reading of Sonnet 73 does not, of course, exhaust its possibilities of meaning. It does demonstrate, however, the New Critical tenet that each poem is unique, and must be examined in and of itself.[10] It is only through an acceptance of each poem's autonomy that the reader can work through the various levels of the poetic text, and disentangle these levels directed to the ostensible addressee from those directed to the ideal reader.

The weakness of New Criticism as a theory, however, is that it fosters an interest in new, original and often ingenious interpretations of texts, particularly of the more familiar texts of the literary canon, at the expense of investigating more thoroughly and systematically the mechanisms and ways by which such interpretations may be arrived at, and may be judged as valid or invalid. The emphasis on the multiplicity of verbal meaning in poetic texts, together with the New Critical interest in irony, paradox and ambiguity, can lead to an evaluation of a poem as good or bad on the basis purely of the degree to which it yields up ironic and paradoxical readings.[11] In short, New Criticism lacks a systematic poetics of reading.[12] The task of evolving such a poetics is taken up by structuralist and post-structuralist theory.

Notes

1.   Not to be confused with Impressionism, a turn-of-the-century school of art which explored the 'impression' of the physical world on the senses. Impressionist painters include such figures as Manet, Pissarro, Cézanne and Gauguin. Debussy is often thought of as an Impressionist composer, creating aurally what the painters accomplished visually.

2.   Conclusion, *The Renaissance: Studies in Art and Poetry* (1873; New York: Mentor-NAL, 1959) 159. All further quotations from Pater refer to this edition.

3.   For an account of *Scrutiny*, its purpose and its importance, see Francis Mulhern, *The Moment of 'Scrutiny'* (London: Verso, 1981).

4.   In some ways, Leavis was the spiritual heir of Matthew Arnold, the nineteenth-century doyen of English cultural values. Like Arnold, Leavis returned again and again to attack what his predecessor, in *Culture and Anarchy*, called Philistinism, that is, the ascendancy of tastes and attitudes which are not only unrefined and uneducated, but which threaten to contaminate and vulgarise the culture at large. For Leavis, however, the Philistines frequently occupy positions of power in the very literary and educational institutions which are supposed to combat such vulgarisations of the moral and intellectual fibre of society. Likewise, Arnold's desire,

expressed in his essay 'The Function of Criticism at the Present Time', that the nation be taught the best that has been thought and said finds its analogue in Leavis' notion of the Great Tradition.

5. Fabian Gudas, 'Organism', *Princeton Encyclopedia of Poetry and Poetics*, ed. Alex Preminger *et al.*, enlarged edition. (London: Macmillan, 1975).

6. For a retrospective defence of New Criticism against commonly made accusations such as the charge of lack of historical perspective, see René Wellek, 'The New Criticism: Pro and Contra', in *The Attack on Literature and Other Essays* 89–103.

7. Cf. Eliot's observation that 'The progress of an artist is a continual self-sacrifice, a continual extinction of personality' ('Tradition and the Individual Talent' 17). Eliot is here speaking of the dialogue of the poet with his or her predecessor-poets, an idea that Harold Bloom has explored further and differently in *The Anxiety of Influence: A Theory of Poetry* (London: OUP, 1973). The idea that the individual poet must merge him or herself with the general idea of 'poet-ness' parallels the requirement that the reader of a poem submerge his or her actual identity in the one constructed by the poetic text. The notion seems to derive, at least partially, from Keats' thesis of 'negative capability'.

8. This is an interesting image, for two reasons. First, the gothic architecture of mediaeval churches derived the shape of its columns from the notion of the tree in a forest of trees: the overarching and interlacing branches of the latter become the decorated arches of the church roof. English perpendicular architecture modified this feature somewhat, but the architectural metaphor remained. Hence, Shakespeare's use of the metaphor is perfectly appropriate.

   Second, after the dissolution of the monasteries by Henry VIII, and the abandonment by England of the Roman Church for Protestantism, many ecclesiastical buildings were allowed to fall into decay and ruin. Bare ruined choirs would have been familiar sights to Shakespeare's contemporaries.

9. It is possible to interpret the second person in the poem as an externalisation of the first, so that the speaker is seen to address himself. Read this way, the couplet asserts and affirms the speaker's reluctance to accept his own decrepitude and death. However, such a reading introduces certain complications. The idea of an externalised self is rather awkward in the quatrains, where the formulations of perception ('thou mayst in me behold,' 'In me thou see'st') seem more naturally to imply a second identity — whether a specific or generalised 'thou' — distinct from the speaker. If this is the case, a no less awkward shift is required in the couplet to produce the externalised self whom the speaker addresses. Though such a shift can be justified by the division of the poem into quatrains and a couplet, so that the speaker appears to turn from addressing another to addressing himself, the assumption of three separate personae (speaker, listener, externalised self) compounds the difficulty of the poem. One could argue that the listener functions for the speaker merely as a surrogate self, one which emerges more clearly towards the end of the sonnet. But this is rather cumbersome, and constructs a scenario not

altogether validated by the text itself (though, of course, it may be possible in the context of the narrative told by Shakespeare's sonnet sequence).

10. See, for example, Elder Olson's analysis of Yeats' poem in '"Sailing to Byzantium": Prolegomena to a Poetics of the Lyric', in which he asserts that the 'argument' of a poem is always *sui generis*, of its own kind.

11. A similar criticism may be levelled at Cleanth Brooks' *Well Wrought Urn*. Brooks tends to justify the reputation of the canonised, traditional poems which he subjects to scrutiny by finding in them the paradox and the irony that the New Critics prize.

12. The *Princeton Encyclopedia of Poetry and Poetics* defines 'poetics' as 'a systematic theory or doctrine of poetry. It defines poetry and its various branches and subdivisions, forms and technical resources, and discusses the principles that govern it and that distinguish it from other creative activities.'

Suggestions for Further Reading

Primary

Abrams, M.H. 'Orientation of Critical Theories'. *The Mirror and the Lamp: Romantic Theory and the Critical Tradition*. 1953. Lodge *20th Century Literary Criticism* 1–26.

Brooks, Cleanth. 'Irony As A Principle of Structure'. 1949. Perry 196–211.

— *Modern Poetry and the Tradition*. Chapel Hill: University of North Carolina Press, 1967.

— *The Well Wrought Urn: Studies in the Structure of Poetry*. New York: Harcourt, Brace and World, 1947.

— and Robert Penn Warren, eds. *Understanding Poetry*. New York: Holt, Rinehart and Winston, 1976.

Brower, Reuben Arthur. *The Fields of Light: An Experiment in Critical Reading*. New York: Galaxy-Oxford University Press, 1962.

Crane, R.S. *The Languages of Criticism and the Structure of Poetry*. Toronto: University of Toronto Press, 1953.

— , W.R. Keast, *et al. Critics and Criticism Ancient and Modern*. Chicago and London: University of Chicago Press, 1952.

Eliot, T.S. *Selected Essays*. 1932. London: Faber, 1966.

Empson, William. *Seven Types of Ambiguity*. 1947. New York: New Directions, 1966.

Leavis, F.R. *The Common Pursuit*. Harmondsworth: Penguin, 1962.

— *New Bearings in English Poetry: A Study of the Contemporary Situation*. 1952. Harmondsworth: Penguin, 1963.

— ed. *A Selection from* Scrutiny. 2 vols. Cambridge: Cambridge University Press, 1968.

Olson, Elder. '"Sailing to Byzantium:" Prolegomena to a Poetics of the Lyric'. 1942. Perry 181–95.

Ransom, John Crowe. 'Criticism, Inc.' *The World's Body*. 1937. Lodge, *20th Century Literary Criticism* 228–39.

Richards, I.A. *Practical Criticism: A Study of Literary Judgment.* London: Routledge, Kegan Paul, 1929.
Tindall, William York. *The Literary Symbol.* Bloomington and London: Indiana University Press, 1955.
Wimsatt, W.K., Jr., and Monroe C. Beardsley. *The Verbal Icon: Studies in the Meaning of Poetry.* Lexington: University of Kentucky Press, 1954.

Secondary

Abrams, M.H. 'New Criticism'. *A Glossary of Literary Terms.* 4th edn. New York: Holt, Rinehart & Winston, 1981. 117–9.
Orsini, G.N.G. 'Poetics'. *Princeton Encyclopedia of Poetry and Poetics.* Eds Alex Preminger, Frank J. Warnke and O.B. Hardison, Jr. London and Basingstoke: Macmillan, 1975.
Robey, David. 'Anglo-American New Criticism'. Jefferson and Robey 65–83.
Wellek, René. *The Attack on Literature and Other Essays.* Brighton: Harvester, 1982.

3

Structuralism

Structuralist literary theory derives from the linguistic theory of the Swiss Ferdinand de Saussure. He was trained in the field of philology, which, during the latter part of the nineteenth century, was dominated by German scholarship.[1] Though this scholarship achieved many important discoveries (for example, the laws historically determining the changes of vowels and consonants in a language), it was essentially descriptive in nature and historical in focus. It did not explain *how* language worked, but merely recorded its evolutionary changes.

In order to explore the nature of language itself, Saussure turned away from historical linguistic study. In the place of the *diachronic* model favoured by the philologists — that is, the study of language across historical periods — Saussure set up a *synchronic* model, which viewed language as related to a culture and its activities at a *single historical moment*.

This move allowed Saussure to postulate two further important points. First, freed from the constraint to regard language from the traditional historical perspective of linguistic evolution, he found that language is a *system* or a *structure*. Second, he concluded that language is the governing model for all other aspects of human perception and activity. Put another way, his linguistic research led to the idea that our perception of reality, and hence also the ways in which we respond to it, are dictated — or constructed — by the structure of the language we speak.

Saussurean structuralism remained largely a speciality of linguists until World War II. In 1941, the French anthropologist Claude Lévi-Strauss took refuge in New York at the New School for Social Research. There he met the Russian linguist Roman Jakobson, whose own work had been influenced by Saussure's theory of language. From him, Lévi-Strauss learned about structuralism, which he then applied to his own field of study. Edmund Leach explains the object of enquiry of structural anthropology thus:[2]

What we know about the external world we apprehend through our senses. The phenomena which we perceive have the characteristics which we attribute to them because of the way our senses operate and the way the human brain is designed to order and interpret the stimuli which are fed into it. One very important feature of this ordering process is that we cut up the continua of space and time with which we are surrounded into segments so that we are predisposed to think of the environment as consisting of vast numbers of separate things belonging to named classes, and to think of the passage of time as consisting of sequences of separate events. Correspondingly, when, as men, we construct artificial things (artifacts of all kinds), or devise ceremonials, or write histories of the past, we imitate our apprehension of Nature: the products of our Culture are segmented and ordered in the same way as we suppose the products of Nature to be segmented and ordered.

It is the task of structural anthropology to discover the patterns or structures by which the experience of reality is segmented, and to show how these patterns and structures function, both individually and in relation to one another.

Lévi-Strauss's anthropological method was taken up in the 1950s by French thinkers and writers. Given the strongly political positions of these intellectuals, structuralism as a theory developed a new political dimension, one which was confirmed by the events of May 1968, when French students made common cause with workers on political and economic issues. In the riots and disturbances that followed, structuralist theory emerged as a powerful rival to the traditional academic approaches, such as historicism, textual scholarship and textual explication. In fact, structuralism became the theory by which the intellectual avant-garde identified itself.

The intellectual ferment of the period produced a number of figures and theories important to contemporary theory in general. These include Louis Althusser's work on Marxist theory, Jacques Lacan's on psychoanalysis, Roland Barthes' on literature and culture, and Michel Foucault's on history and the structure of knowledge.[3] However, in recent years structuralism has become less significant in France, while developing a following in the English-speaking world. Edmund Leach has been a principal figure in the field of linguistics in England, while Jonathan Culler has been important in the dissemination of literary structuralist theory and method in the United States.

Structuralist theory assumes that literature, as an artefact of the culture, is modelled on the structure of language, which is deemed to construct the very nature of our perceptions of reality. This premiss leads to two important consequences. First, it permits structuralist theory to investigate the ways in which literary texts are structured like language — their grammar, as it were. Inevitably, this paves the way for a semiotic emphasis upon *how* a text means, in place of the *what* favoured by New Criticism.

Second, if language provides the model for all human perception and activity, literature can be examined as a system in relation to others within a particular culture, since all are assumed to be founded on the linguistic model. This model being granted, the emphasis on semiosis in the structuralist approach to poetry implies also an interest in the way in which texts reflect or imitate perceived reality. The traditional concern with mimesis in literary texts can thus be integrated into structuralism's essentially semiotic focus.

We have already observed that, while New Criticism addresses itself principally to the semiosis of the poetic text, it also includes an interest in its mimetic qualities. The situation or moment described in the poem, the emotions implied or explicitly named and defined, and so on, are assumed to reflect the state of things in reality, not as a simple transcription or reflection of real events, but as a representation of the way in which things work and inter-relate in reality. Structuralism makes certain similar assumptions, but for very different reasons, and arrives at very different conclusions.

The two consequences of the linguistic premiss lead to further fruitful investigation. In terms of the first, literary study is enabled to turn to the question of poetics, that is, the analysis of the *processes of meaning* and their relation to form, in place of the New Critical insistence on interpretation. Indeed, Jonathan Culler remarks in this connection that we need fewer interpretations of literary texts, and more inquiry into how interpretation takes place in the readers' minds as they interact with the text (*The Pursuit of Signs* 3–17).

The second consequence enables us to integrate the object of our study more firmly into the structure of the culture at large, including its social, historical and economic dimensions. Though, as we have seen, the New Critics do not deny this relation of literature to other elements in the culture, they tend to stress the uniqueness of the literary text as a means to harmonise and unify cultural discord and discontinuity. Literary language becomes a special means by which this may be accomplished. The effect of this is to isolate literature as a domain separate from other activities in the culture.

The structuralist assumption of the primacy of language as a semiotic structure and of its role in cultural activity of all sorts accomplishes the harmonising function accorded to literature by New Criticism. If language is the first-order system of signification, all others can be treated as second-order systems, and unified under the sign of language itself.

This assumption naturally leads to an enquiry into the ways in which these second-order systems model the first-order system, and the ways in which they differ from one another. Literary study thus becomes an investigation into the nature of language as used by literature, compared with other forms of verbal communication in the culture. Structuralist criticism therefore looks at literature in two ways. In the first, literature is examined as a system or structure in itself, in order to determine its characteristic patterns, and to discover the laws by which these permit meaning to be made. In the second, the literary system is situated within wider cultural and linguistic systems. This placement also affects the way in which meaning is made in particular literary texts. Understanding the semiosis of a text implies a grasp of its mimetic qualities, since these are likewise founded on a primary model of language.

Jean Piaget observes that 'the notion of structure is comprised of three key ideas: the idea of wholeness, the idea of transformation, and the idea of self-regulation' (5). Any structure is made up of *elements* — for example, in the case of poetry, words — and the *laws or codes* which govern these, and combine them into a whole. These two constituents of a structure occur or exist simultaneously: we do not get first the elements, and then the laws, or first the laws, then the elements. Elements may be combined into different structures by different laws. Take the example of the alphabet and a poem. Both are made up of the same fundamental elements, letters or characters, but the laws that govern each do so to different ends, and thus create different structures.

Two important laws in this connection are those of *relation* and of *opposition*. As a general rule, we tend to assume that the language we use has essential, absolute or 'real' meaning, and points directly to objects, signs and sounds in the real world. The example of the alphabet, however, shows us that meaning emerges from relations *within the system*. Take the letter A, for instance. By itself, it is, at best, ambiguous in meaning; at worst, it is meaningless. It gains meaning *only when it is related to other similar elements in the same system*. In the alphabet, these may be defined as vowels (A has meaning when seen in relation to the other vowels E, I, O, U, to which it is similar); or as consonants (A has meaning when seen as opposed to B, C, D, F, G, and so on, consonants being a different category); or as placement in the traditional order of the alphabet (A has meaning in relation or in opposition to Z).

The law of relation allows us to perceive analogies or connections between elements, although we should be aware that these analogies of signification are always *differential*: the fact that two elements are seen to be related does not mean that they are therefore to be identified with one another. A may be *like* E, in that both are vowels; but A is *not the same as* E.

This brings us to the second law, the law of opposition. This constitutes meaning by exclusion, in allowing us to define one element as *different from* (not merely contradictory of) *another in the system*: A has meaning because it is *not* B or E or Z. These two laws, therefore, work together in the process of making meaning in a structure. They cannot function independently of one another. In this way, they demonstrate, at a different level, the structuralist notion of the wholeness of the system.

The category in which an element may be classified is called a *paradigm*, and, as our example of the letter A shows, an element may appear in several paradigms simultaneously. In the case of our example, A appears in the large paradigm of the alphabet, and in the lesser paradigms of vowel, non-consonant, and first-last ordering. There are other paradigms that we can no doubt think of in which A can be placed; and probably we can think of many other examples of elements which can be located in several paradigms at the same time. The important thing to remember is that the paradigm functions like a list of possibilities. We choose, consciously or unconsciously, from a number of paradigms as we construct or analyse a statement. What we choose is given meaning, according to the laws of relation and opposition, by the paradigm drawn from, as opposed to other paradigms which we have rejected, and by the elements within that paradigm *not* selected.

When elements come to be combined into more complex organisations, a *syntagm* is created. The relation of paradigm to syntagm is best visualised as a vertical list of possibilities from which a unit is drawn to be combined with others, according to the appropriate laws or codes, into a 'horizontal', that is, linear or serial, utterance:

p	p	p	p	p	p	p
a	a	a	a	a	a	a
r	r	r	r	r	r	r
a	a	a	a	a	a	a
S	Y	N	T	A	G	M
d	d	d	d	d	d	d
i	i	i	i	i	i	i
g	g	g	g	g	g	g
m	m	m	m	m	m	m

With the formation of a syntagmatic text, other laws are called into play. Again, these make sense only within the relevant system. For example, the way in which a poem is set out on the page typographically is very like the way in which an algebraic equation is set out (excluding, of course, the very different symbols used in either kind of text, poetic or algebraic). We *read* these texts differently, however, because we know that they belong to different structures, and therefore have different laws. We expect an equation to follow a process of mathematical logic, and to conclude with a 'right' or 'wrong' result: it is self-checking in a fairly obvious way. The reading of a poem, on the other hand, is notoriously less susceptible of a 'right' or 'wrong' result at the end, and to determine whether as a structure it is self-checking requires us to appeal to laws other than those of mathematical logic.

The example of the meaning of A in the alphabet shows us that in a structure, the elements co-exist *simultaneously*, even though we may come to know them only through a sequence of time. Thus, A is the first letter of the alphabet, and derives some meaning from that fact alone. Any other meaning this letter may have depends on *sets of relationships* within the system. To take another example, B gains signification not merely because it is the second letter in the alphabet, or because it is a consonant, whereas A is not, though these are important differentiations. But B also has meaning in the language system by virtue of its relation to sounds which are linguistically similar in production, but which are in fact capable of producing very different meanings. For instance, B and P are, as sounds, technically related to V and F, because all four are produced in the area of the lips, and are either voiced or unvoiced. The technical linguistic details are less important here than the recognition that, in English, these sounds are *distinctive*. If we combine each of them with *-at*, we actually produce different meanings for each sound group. *Bat, pat, fat* and *vat*, regardless of the similarity of their linguistic production, have very different significations in English. (These *distinctive features* are not always the same in all languages. In Spanish, for example, B and V are not as clearly opposed, resulting in pronunciations of words which sound distinctly different to non-Spanish ears, but which, to a Spanish speaker, may have the same meaning.)

In poetry, the matter is, of course, much more complicated. First, there are the sets of relations and distinctive features common to all utterances in the language; these are opposed in turn to an aspect that may be called 'poetic', though by this we should not understand merely the eighteenth-century notion of poetic diction, appropriate to poetry only. A useful way of understanding this notion is to be found in the theory of Roman Jakobson: the *poetic function* foregrounds the language itself of the text; it emphasises 'the message for its own sake' ('Linguistics and Poetics' in DeGeorge and DeGeorge 93). Jakobson warns, however, that this cannot be divorced from the other functions of communication; nor is poetry the only kind of text which employs the poetic function.

The reading of poetic texts, then, must first be seen in a correct relation to the reading of more ordinary texts. The opposition of poetic language to the language of other acts of communication lies in the degree of self-consciousness of the language itself. Features such as rhyme, rhythm, repetitions of words, phrases or images draw the reader's attention *away* from any reference to the context of reality, and *towards* the text itself. Under the influence of the poetic function, the text becomes *self-referential*.

Another element operating at the level of wholeness in the structure of poetry is that of the poetic *system*. We become aware, as we read one poem, of how it resembles or defines itself against others, in terms of theme, treatment or language. This feature is called *intertextuality*, and is one of the ways by which we come to know the structure of poetry as a genre. The very first time we read or hear a poem, we may have difficulty coming to terms with it, but by the second time, we already have some intertextual knowledge about the way it works or sounds. As with other kinds of system, the principle of the completeness of the structure operates, even though we come to know it only slowly, and after reading many poetic texts.

Finally, there is the structure or system set up within an individual poetic text. Sets of relations and of oppositions are part of this, and to understand the text as a whole, the reader must look for these sets. This method of reading does not, like New Criticism, look immediately for an interpretation of the poem; rather, it seeks instead those structures or patterns that permit such a reading. These create what Culler calls the 'empty meaning' in the text (*Structuralist Poetics* 119), which is then available to be 'filled' with the more substantive meanings permitted by the actual semantic and lexical content of the text.

The notion of the wholeness of a structure, then, is an important one. It defines the structure as existing in all its aspects simultaneously, though we as readers often apprehend these only sequentially. It is important to note that there is a certain similarity between the structuralist concept of wholeness of system, and the New Critical idea of the totality of the text. However, where the New Critical approach leads to a view of the text as almost a spatial aesthetic object, structuralist theory sees design or structure in a text as an abstraction which is embodied in or manifested by the actual linguistic syntagm. Moreover, it shows that an individual text not only has its own structure, constituted by sets of oppositions and relations, but that it is itself part of a larger structure.

However, if we were to stop with the idea of wholeness alone, we would end up with a rather static notion of structure. Its chief characteristic would be *synchrony*, that is, existing or functioning only at a single temporal moment. We would be led to one of two mistaken conclusions. The first would be that structures never change, and that the synchronic moment is an enormous one, stretching from the earliest records of humanity to the present day. Second, if we were to accept that history is the record of changes, we would be driven to assume, as an alternative conclusion, that change in structures occurs in a dislocated, jerky fashion, one discrete and independent structure following another.

In reality, of course, structures neither exist unchanged forever, nor give way suddenly to other new and totally unrelated ones. Indeed, one of the weaknesses in Saussure's theory is that it favours synchrony over diachrony. Yet structure is in effect a dynamic concept, and its theorisation should allow for the idea that change takes place constantly and often imperceptibly over time. One structure *becomes* the successor to another. A principle of transformation is thus necessary to redefine structure as *diachronic*, that is, as occurring between historical moments.

This principle of transformation is the means by which a system may accept or exclude new elements. The exclusion of a new element will usually imply that the structure maintains its status quo, whereas the acceptance is likely to require a rearrangement of the elements in the system, according to its central laws of relation and opposition (Piaget 11). This principle leads us from the individual text to the system of which the text is a part. Of course, once a poem is written in its final form, it remains fixed as a text. However, it may well affect the literary and, specifically, the poetic system. The first sonnet ever, for example, introduced a new genre into the poetic system, and thereby altered it. Subsequent development of the sonnet form made further changes, not only in the poetic system, but also in the subsystem created by the sonnet form itself.[4]

Moreover, the ways in which a text may be read will depend on the condition of both the literary system and the larger cultural one at the time of reading. This necessarily implies that one reader's perception of certain elements in a text, to the exclusion of others, will produce a meaning different from that of a reader at another moment in history. This, too, is an example of the principle of transformation in operation.

This principle, then, allows a structure to grow and to develop novelties of form, rescuing it from immobility in historical terms, and from monotony in conceptual ones. This suggests, however, that there must be a further principle in the very idea of structure that works to preserve the integrity of a structure, even as it changes, in order to prevent its simply becoming dissipated through lack of order and identity. Piaget defines this principle as that of self-regulation.

The laws that pertain to the self-regulation of a system can be thought of as defining a particular kind of paradigm. In order for an item to belong to one paradigm rather than another, the limits of the paradigm must, in the first place, be identifiable so that the nature of the group that it classifies or names is both clear and knowable. In the second place, that autonomy of identity must be related to any other relevant paradigms. Often, one system of classification turns out to be a subset of a larger, broader and thus vaguer system, or it may include subsets that need to be defined more carefully. Thus, in our alphabetical example above, the letter A belongs in the paradigm of vowels, which is a subset of the paradigm of the alphabet itself. Poetry may likewise be defined as a subset of the literary system, and the sonnet 'system' as a subset of the poetic.

The function of these limitations of identity is twofold. They define more clearly which elements may be included in the system, and which are to be excluded. This very principle of inclusion or exclusion of elements assists in providing a way of closing the system, so that we know when we have exceeded the limits of one system, or when we are dealing with a different structure altogether. If we consider the nature of the letter A as a symbol of primacy or firstness of position, we can see that in this aspect of the possible significations of alphabetical letters, we are close to a different system of ordering elements, that of numbers. That this is so is evident in the way in which alphabetical letters are used in only a limited way to denote order: we use the opposition of A and Z frequently, to signify firstness and lastness of order, and, if we are listing a few points we might use the first few letters of the alphabet to indicate order. But to use alphabetical symbols for a large number of points might lead to confusion. Consider, for instance, what would happen once we reached Z in a list of 30 points.

The three principles enunciated by Piaget, therefore, enable us to see a poem as itself constituting an individual system, complete in all its parts, but also as part of larger systems: in ascending order, those of poetry, literary language and ordinary language. The principles of transformation and self-regulation may at first sight appear paradoxical, since the first implies an open system, whereas the second a closed one. We might take, as an example to deal with this apparent contradiction, the form of the sonnet. In its development in the later Middle Ages and during the Renaissance, this lyric form evolved as a 14-line poem, with certain preferred rhyming and metrical schemes. We might say that this particular form, in being typical of the sonnet, reveals the laws of self-regulation. However, both during the later Renaissance, and, later still, in the nineteenth-century, experiments in the sonnet form to expand the number of lines indicate the principle of transformation. The sonnet system is enabled to change what appears to be an immutable shape.

Nevertheless, the principle of self-regulation remains a powerful factor, since a 16-line poem is not necessarily a sonnet. Other elements must exist in the form to enable Gerard Manley Hopkins's $14\frac{1}{2}$ and 15-line sonnets, as well as George Meredith's 16-line ones, to remain definable as *sonnets*. One such structural element is the 'turn' or reversal at the end of the poem. This typically occurs in many Renaissance poems at the ninth line, as we observed in discussing the Shakespeare sonnet in the preceding chapter. However, in the so-called English or Shakespearean forms, it is often delayed until the thirteenth and fourteenth lines. In the longer sonnet form such as that favoured by Meredith, the turn is likewise kept in reserve until the fifteenth and sixteenth lines. This, however, appears to be near the limit of definition of the sonnet as a form. If the sonnet were to be sustained to, say, 24 lines, it would be much more difficult, since the effect of the turn depends on the brevity of the form. The reversal needs to be close to the opening of the sonnet in order to be perceived as a reversal.

Thus, if changes occur in a system, laws intrinsic to it permit some changes and not others; they also allow change to a certain point, but not beyond. Otherwise, there could be no system, and change would be endless and indecipherable.

The structuralist enterprise in literature presumes three dimensions in the individual literary texts with which it is concerned. The first is that of the text as a particular system or structure in itself. The text is here deemed to use language in ways which are characteristic of that text alone. Thus, words may take on shadings of meaning which the context alone prompts; further, these words are organised into grammatical, semantic and formal structures which need to be uncovered by the reader, and examined in order to determine what kind of meaning he or she may make in the text, as well as how that meaning is to be made. Another way of putting this is to say that each poem has its own 'grammar', 'syntax' and 'vocabulary' which define the way its use of language is to be decoded and understood.

The second dimension of the individual text is that which situates it within the literary system as a whole. The presence of such a system necessarily means that texts are unavoidably influenced, in terms of both their formal and conceptual structures, by other texts.[5] Part of the meaning of any text, as a consequence, depends on its *intertextual relation* to other texts, both contemporary and earlier ones. This includes not only such generic matters as the formal structure of a poem — say, whether it is a sonnet or an elegy — but also the meanings of symbols and metaphors, as well as the kinds of diction typically associated with poetic texts.

The third dimension of the individual text is that which relates it to the culture as a whole. This aspect will be addressed in later chapters in this book. All that needs to be said here is that structuralist criticism which foregrounds this particular aspect of the poem tends, of necessity, to emphasise the mimetic, as opposed to the purely semiotic, focus of structuralist theory.

All three dimensions of the structuralist investigation are directed particularly at the reader's activity in the text. As with New Criticism, the role of the author is set aside in the process of making meaning in the text. The New Critics evacuated the text of authorial presence because they argued that historical and biographical concerns were not relevant to the text's meaning as a verbal structure, and because authorial intent was either embodied in the text, or it was entirely irrelevant to its meaning.

The structuralist argument rests on very different assumptions. The first is that of language, and its primary role in human and social activity. Language is, of course, the public property of the members of any culture, and this fact may lead one to the New Critical conclusion that the reader's manipulation of language in confronting a text is as valid as the author's in constructing it. However, the structuralist principle that our perception of reality is conditioned and mediated by language means that we are trapped in and by language — indeed, Fredric Jameson calls it 'the prison-house of language'. This suggests that imposed upon us, as a fact of daily existence, is the need to decode or 'read' texts of different kinds. The process of reading becomes paramount because it is the way we make sense not only of literary texts, but also of reality and the lives we live. The function of literary author, granted a special status by Romantic and post-Romantic convention, may be seen from this perspective simply as an early stage in the genesis of meaning in a text. That function is complemented and completed by the more important function of the reader. The process of literary creation is therefore explained in structuralist theory by the hypothesis that the author of a text is also its first reader.

Because authors are readers also of 'texts' of many different kinds by other 'authors', the working of the principle of intertextuality in any given text becomes complicated and subtle. Intertextual reference extends not only through the diachronic dimension of meaning, but also through the synchronic. Thus, the author becomes a channel for cultural preoccupations and concerns. In a way, the culture writes the literary text by means of the author.

This demotion of the author from the privileged status of creator to the lower rank of cultural medium attacks a central part of the mythology of literature and of literary study. It is far more radical than the setting aside of the author by the New Critics as a necessary element in the production of literary texts, but an irrelevant one in their reading. Moreover, it shifts attention away from the mystique of authorial inspiration, and moves it instead towards the processes by which readers make sense, in different ways, of literary texts.

To think in structuralist terms about poetry as system is to see it as a linguistic system operating at several levels. First, there is the level of *language* itself: the text must be readable as a syntactic and grammatical structure. Next, there is the level of *poetic language*: the grammar and the syntax (and sometimes the diction or vocabulary) characteristically used in individual poetic texts. Third, there is the *grammar of poetry* as the genre in which these individual texts may be situated. Finally, there is the *grammar of literary works in general*, of which the genre of poetry is a component. At each new level, the linguistic structure is transformed into a different element, moving from, say, a fundamental grammar at one level to a vocabulary element in another.

Seeing literary structure as functioning at different levels in this way helps the structuralist critic, like the New Critic, to define literature as a verbal construct different from other verbal constructs, like conversation, to take an oral example, or like a letter to a newspaper, to take a written one. Further, it also helps to clarify the nature of a single system — in our case, that of poetry. Conceiving of poetry thus also helps us to see literary works as falling into particular genres or kinds, each one defined by its own laws and conventions. Likewise, the notion of a larger literary system gives individual works a sense of context which includes a historical perspective that may suggest how that work is to be read.

Structuralism in Practice

Lewis Carroll's nonsense poem 'Jabberwocky' provides an instructive text on which to practise the principles of structuralist criticism. Its nonsensicality derives less from absurdity of situation and character (as is the case, for example, with much of the nonsense verse of Edward Lear, or, indeed, with other Carrollian whimsies, such as the White Knight's Song in *Through the Looking Glass*) than from the deployment of a vocabulary which Carroll himself invented, and which therefore remains opaque to the reader. Because we are thus deprived of clear referents for the text, we are forced, if we wish to try and make sense of the poem, to attend to the structures which both underlie it and which relate it intertextually to other texts:

Jabberwocky

'Twas brillig, and the slithy toves
   Did gyre and gimble in the wabe;
All mimsy were the borogoves,
   And the mome raths outgrabe.

'Beware the Jabberwock, my son!
   The jaws that bite, the claws that catch!
Beware the Jubjub bird, and shun
   The frumious Bandersnatch!'

He took his vorpal sword in hand;
   Long time the manxome foe he sought —
So rested he by the Tumtum tree,
   And stood awhile in thought.

And, as in uffish thought he stood,
   The Jabberwock, with eyes of flame,
Came whiffling through the tulgey wood,
   And burbled as it came!

One, two! One, two! And through and through
   The vorpal blade went snicker-snack!
He left it dead, and with its head
   He came galumphing back.

'And hast thou slain the Jabberwock?
   Come to my arms, my beamish boy!
O frabjous day! Callooh! Callay!'
   He chortled in his joy.

'Twas brillig, and the slithy toves
   Did gyre and gimble in the wabe;
All mimsy were the borogoves,
   And the mome raths outgrabe.

We may divide the problem of meaning in this poem into two categories. The first, as we have noted above, is the question of the language used by Carroll, and how we can relate strange words like 'brillig' to our own experience of language. The second category is the question of the meaning of the poem's structure or design, and is clearly contingent to some degree on our arriving at an answer to the first question.

A careful consideration of 'Jabberwocky' suggests that, though we may not possess the precise meaning of each word in the text, the rules of English grammar and syntax allow us to hazard fairly useful guesses at the approximate meaning of the unfamiliar words. 'Wabe', for instance, coming in what appears to be an adverbial phrase of place (in the wabe), suggests a location of some sort; on the other hand, the plural 'mome raths', combined with a Germanic sort of verb (outgrabe), implies that these are creatures engaged in activity of some kind.

However, the strategy of making purely grammatical and syntactical meaning of the text does not lead to a satisfying decoding of the poem's lexical content, because the text will permit us only to sketch in an approximate area of potential meaning, leaving the centre, what the word actually signifies, blank or empty. In fact, the actual lexical 'meaning' may not be as pertinent here as in other poetic texts. Because 'Jabberwocky' forces us continually to confront a text for whose key words we have no meaning, part of its signification may be a confrontation with the problem of language itself, the questions of referentiality and signification. In this case, we may conclude that whatever a 'wabe' or 'mome raths' might 'really' mean, that meaning is secondary to a desire manifested in the text to play with the rules of language. That these rules are observed is evidenced by such examples as agreement of number between subject and verb ('borogoves' takes the plural 'were'), and that adverbs and adjectives remain relatively recognisable in form and syntactical position in the sentence ('mimsy' is clearly a description of 'borogoves', as 'mome' is of 'raths').

We may take a further step, and decide that the nonsense words in 'Jabberwocky' are very evidently self-referential in meaning. However, we cannot, in this case, claim that the text actually defines the meaning of the obscure words. The issue of exact lexical meaning is thus either irrelevant in the case of this text, or else is indefinitely postponed in the process of making meaning of the poem. Later in *Through the Looking Glass*, Alice recites the poem to Humpty Dumpty, and asks him to explain the text to her. The meanings which are offered to her for the 'hard words' reinforces their essential self-referentiality, for Humpty Dumpty's fairly arbitrary assignment of meaning indicates that we as readers must also hazard guesses. The text itself offers few clues and no guarantees to aid us in our task of discovering the meaning of the poem.

The second category of meaning is the structure of the text itself. An analysis of this shows that it has two parts. The first consists of an opening stanza which is repeated identically at its close. However, the relation of these two identical stanzas to the remaining five, in terms of the poem's meaning, is not made clear. The first and last stanzas stand in a paratactic relation to the inner stanzas of the poem: that is, it is a relation only of contiguity or adjacence, rather than of causality or sequentiality, or of some other logical relationship (Smith 98–109). Our codes of reading, however, invite us to assume some kind of important connection between the repeated stanza and the rest of the poem, and hence some significant meaning in its presence. Accordingly, therefore, as readers we will be inclined to *construct* and *insert* a meaningful relationship in order to make sense of what would otherwise be a casually chaotic text.

We may thus reach a variety of conclusions regarding the meaning of the repeated stanza and its relation to the rest of the poem. One such conclusion might be that the two stanzas serve as a frame for the inner ones. In that case, the repetition is at once both introductory and closural (see Smith, especially 158–66). This is, in effect, to argue the meaning of the two stanzas from their function. Another conclusion might be that the repeated stanza exists in a kind of negative relationship to the rest of the poem: in other words, its meaning is, precisely, its irrelevance to the remainder of the text. Yet another argument might be that these two stanzas act as an ironic commentary on action described in the central ones. This is the possibility which we shall now explore.

In the second part of the poem, the five middle stanzas, a story is told, though its antecedents and its consequences remain undisclosed to us. We are not told why the boy goes off to slay the Jabberwock, nor are we told what the implications of this act might be. However, familiarity with intertexts such as epic poetry and mediaeval romance suggests that such quests mark rites of passage, and the coming of age of the hero. This hero seems to be a little unready for his responsibilities, being taken almost unawares by the monstrous Jabberwock, still, apparently, under the tutelage of the speaker of the stanzas.

The inconsequentiality of the act of slaying the Jabberwock in itself points to a process of irony at work in the poem. However, within the structure of the text, and in its bifurcation into functioning parts, we can see further irony at work. Let us consider the way each of these constructs the concept of time in the poem. Time in the repeated stanza is static. The events described (whatever their precise 'meaning') recur at the same time, in the same order, and to the same effect. On the other hand, time in the central five stanzas is dynamic. A story is told, and a sequence of actions is accomplished. Indeed, it is in this opposition of static and dynamic temporal paradigms that much of the difficulty of meaning in 'Jabberwocky' is to be found. In order to tell a story intelligibly, with plot and action, the text utilises a relatively greater proportion of recognisable signifiers. We may not know what a Jabberwock is, nor what 'vorpal' means, but the fact that the Jabberwock is a monster is made clear in the context, while 'vorpal' appears to be less essential to the meaning than the words it qualifies, 'sword' and 'blade', whose sense is, of course, well known. On the other hand, in the repeated stanza, in which nothing much happens, twice, it is the effect of stasis that is necessary, not the meanings of the individual words. The relatively greater number in these two stanzas, together with their very obscurity, in fact prevents us from attempting to turn them into much more than a background setting.

There are two ways in which we can make sense of this poem, in terms of the dual construction of time in the text. The first way of reading the repetition of temporal stasis in the first and last stanzas is to understand it as the completion of a cycle. The text returns, at the end, to the condition of existence with which it began. Such a reading of course reinforces the closural effect of this repetition, but it also leads us to an understanding of the two parts of the poem as essentially irrelevant to each other. If the cycle of existence is merely resumed, without any change in the world described in the text, and without any recognition of the facts of the boy's achievement and of the Jabberwock's death, then the boy's quest is essentially empty. It has no impact on the way reality is structured in the poem, and hence little value, except for the participants in the quest, namely, the speaker of the central stanzas, the boy and, naturally, the Jabberwock itself.

In the second way, the moment described at the end of the poem may be read not merely as a repetition of the moment described at the beginning, but, instead, as *identical with it*. Read this way, the text appears to describe an instant in time during which two sequences of events, one ordinary and the other extraordinary, take place simultaneously: at the same time that the mome raths outgribe and the toves gyre in the wabe, the beamish boy sets out on his quest and achieves his goal. This reading sets up as an opposition paradigms of the routine and of the unusual, but in such a way, through the paratactic structure, as to suggest the irrelevance of the one to the other. In the world of the mundane, time is measured in regular portions: the opening phrase, 'Twas brillig', using as it does the indeterminate 'it', suggests a location of time, whether 'brillig' denotes a measure of time — for example, 'it was 12 o'clock' — or a condition of nature at a particular moment — for instance, 'it was sunny'. Events in this context occur routinely in relation to the cycles of time ('... and the slithy toves/ Did gyre and gimble in the wabe ...'). On the other hand, in the world of monsters and questing heroes, time is calculated according to individual acts and unpredictable events ('Long time the manxome foe he sought ...'; 'He left it dead, and with its head/ He went galumphing back'). These two worlds are incompatible with each other, and their co-existence in a text which ostensibly unites them serves to highlight their essential differences from one another.

The poem rests, then, upon a series of oppositions. In their construction of time, and in the kind of language used, as well as in their foregrounding of plural and hence generalised references to the various creatures which inhabit the poem (toves, borogoves and raths), the first and last stanzas are opposed, as we have seen, to the central five, which focus on the unique and the individual, both in identity and in action. Within these latter stanzas, we can perceive other oppositional paradigms: youth and age (the boy and the speaker, who in addressing the hero as 'my son' identifies himself as older metaphorically, if not factually); subject and object (speaker and thing or person spoken of); the static and the dynamic (the speaker remains behind, the boy goes out to fight a monster); the extraordinary and the ordinary (a quest for monsters, as opposed to remaining at home, as the speaker evidently does); and so on. The poem's structure thus establishes sets of meaningful *relationships*, even though it may withhold the precise signification of particular words. Yet, in the final analysis, the poem defies any attempt to unify it and make it a totality: any reading of the text runs up against the problem of the relation of the first and last stanzas to the rest of the poem. It is from this dislocation of the text's beginning and ending from its middle that a good deal of the poem's 'nonsensicality' derives, rather than from mere lexical strangeness.

A reader familiar with the literature popular during Carroll's day will recognise in the five central stanzas intertextual allusions in 'Jabberwocky', first, to the literary ballad, and, second, to the story of the quest. Both of these had been popularised by the Romantic poets and their successors. Coleridge's *The Rime of the Ancient Mariner*, and Keats's 'La Belle Dame Sans Merci' and 'The Eve of St Agnes' provide examples of such Romantic poems, which in turn functioned as models for Victorian poems such as Browning's 'Childe Harold'. Such models had already been satirised by Byron in *Don Juan*.

The story of the beamish boy who slays the Jabberwock, then returns with its head to the speaker of the five internal stanzas is clearly a further parody of such poems. Not only do the unfamiliar words tend to defuse the aura of mystery and suspense common to such poems (who, for instance, could seriously fear a creature called the Jubjub bird?), but the hero's actions themselves are less than heroic: he is almost caught napping by the Jabberwock, and his 'galumphing' return suggests an awkward youth rather than a glorious hero. The speaker's response to the boy's success is almost senile — 'O frabjous day! Callooh! Callay!' This, together with the references to the hero as 'my son' and 'my beamish boy', suggest that the speaker is an older man, certainly in a paternal relationship to the hero, if not actually his father. However, aside from the fairly obvious warnings he offers the hero, he displays none of the traits of wisdom or of special knowledge which such figures traditionally exhibit in texts dealing with quests and derring-do. (Compare, for example, such figures as Athene and Virgil, in the quest poems of Homer and Dante, or of Angela, the old nurse, in 'The Eve of St Agnes'.)

This raises another key question: is the speaker of the quest stanzas the same as the speaker of the stanzas with which the poem begins and ends? The scene and activities described therein, as we have seen, have no apparent relevance to the story told in stanzas two to six. Indeed, their function is twofold: to open and close the poem, and to provide a background for the quest-story. Further, we may say that this dual function is intended to conceal the arbitrariness with which the quest begins — with a warning which has no lead-up or explanation — and the inconclusiveness of its conclusion. We are left with an image of the speaker chortling in his joy, and no further mention is made of the hero.

These features imply that the story of the quest is, in the final analysis, simply irrelevant. The repetition of scene and events in the last stanza calls into question the value of the heroic deeds recounted in the preceding stanzas, since they do not affect the text's world as it is constructed in the first stanza, and as it continues to function in the last. We may go so far as to say that in this poem Carroll implicitly criticises, through parody, the literary values of his society, and, through these, stigmatises its ethical ideals as adolescent virtues.

The above reading of 'Jabberwocky' shows the strength of structuralist theory in uncovering the mechanisms in the text by means of which meaning is produced by the reader. Indeed, a New Critical reading would be hard-put to arrive at a satisfying interpretation of this text, given the elusive nature of its language.

On the other hand, New Criticism as a literary theory is centred especially on poetry. It deals less completely with the larger textual structures of prose fiction and drama. Contemporary structuralist theory, by contrast, favours narrative, at the expense of lyric poetry, and the narrative element in 'Jabberwocky' of course responds particularly well, as we have seen, to a structuralist reading. The emergence of contemporary structuralism from a marriage of linguistics with anthropology may be responsible particularly for the emphasis on narrative, since the former discipline interests itself in sequential utterance, and the latter in myth and behaviour. Lyric poetry has tended, until recently, to be dismissed by structuralist theory as merely an instance of the special use of language, Jakobson's poetic function (see, for example, Robert Scholes: 'Poetry celebrates the unique in a culture, a language, a man's way of using his language' [62]).

However, Eugene Vance argues that the narrative model devised by A.-J. Greimas can also be used to explain certain details in the lyrics of twelfth-century France. This view opens up the study of lyric poetry to include narrative codes hitherto excluded, and suggests that the process of making meaning in such texts goes beyond simply marking a particular psychological moment in an implied ongoing sequence of events, but actually *creates* a structure of events within the text of the poem itself.[6]

Structuralist theory, then, is valuable in its ability to expose the patterns and dynamics by which a reader makes meaning in a text. What it is less successful in achieving is actually interpreting the text, as New Criticism does, in order to find not only textual meaning, but also aesthetic, moral and social values. On the other hand, structuralism opens up the text to a variety of ways of reading, and, by insisting on its open-ended nature, extends the practices of reading and criticism beyond the range available to the New Critics. The strong linguistic and textual base of structuralist criticism adds a dimension missing in New Criticism. It is that same base which, however, leads, in the post-structuralist theory of deconstruction, to the exposure of texts as structures of illusory meaning.

Notes

1. The term 'structuralism' itself was coined by Roman Jakobson to describe the theoretical work of the Prague Linguistic Circle in the late 1920s and the 1930s. See the chapter below on Russian Formalism.
2. *Lévi-Strauss* (London: Fontana, 1972) 21.
3. Foucault's contribution is discussed briefly in Chapter 6, Poetry and History.
4. Cf. Eliot's observation that the literary tradition both affects and is affected by the individual work:

   > The existing monuments form an ideal order among themselves, which is modified by the introduction of the new (the really new) work of art among them. The existing order is complete before the new work arrives; for order to persist after the supervention of novelty, the *whole* existing order must be, if ever so slightly, altered; and so the relations, proportions, values of each work of art toward the whole are readjusted ...' ('Tradition and the Individual Talent', *Selected Essays*. London: Faber, 1966, 15).

   The crucial differences between this New Critical statement and the premises of structuralist theory lie, first, in Eliot's assumption of a canon of original works; and, second, in his requirement that the individual work itself be original and innovative. Structuralism, by contrast, assumes simply a body of previous texts, some of which are original and innovative, many of which are not.
5. Cf. Eliot's remarks about the poet's place in the literary tradition in 'Tradition and the Individual Talent', referred to in Note 7, Chapter 2.
6. See also David Buchbinder, 'True-Speaking Flattery: Narrativity and Authenticity in the Sonnet Sequence', *Poetics* 17 (1988): 37–47.

Suggestions for Further Reading

Primary

Barthes, Roland. 'The Death of the Author'. Lodge, *Modern Criticism* 167–72.
— 'The Imagination of the Sign'. Rylance 86–9.
— 'The Struggle with the Angel'. Rylance 90–100.
— 'To Write: An Intransitive Verb?' Rice and Waugh 42–51.
— 'What Is Criticism?' Rylance 82–5.
Benveniste, Emile. 'The Nature of the Linguistic Sign'. Rylance 77–81.
De Man, Paul. 'The Dead-End of Formalist Criticism'. Rylance 101–9.
De Saussure, Ferdinand. 'The Object of Study' and 'Nature of the Linguistic Sign'. Lodge, *Modern Criticism* 2–14.
DeGeorge, Richard T., and Fernande M. DeGeorge, eds. *The Structuralists from Marx to Lévi-Strauss*. Garden City, NY: Doubleday-Anchor, 1972.
Genette, Gérard. 'Structuralism and Literary Criticism'. Lodge, *Modern Criticism* 63–78.
MacCabe, Colin. 'Language, Linguistics and the Study of Literature'. Lodge, *Modern Criticism* 432–44.
Piaget, Jean. *Structuralism*. 1968. Trans. Chaninah Maschler. London: Routledge, 1971.
Robey, David, ed. *Structuralism: An Introduction*. Wolfson College Lectures, 1972. Oxford: Clarendon, 1973.
Selden, Raman. 'Structuralist Theories'. 52–71.
Smith, Barbara Herrnstein. *Poetic Closure: A Study of How Poems End*. Chicago and London: University of Chicago Press, 1968.

Secondary

Abrams, M.H. 'Structuralist Criticism'. *A Glossary of Literary Terms*. 4th edn. New York: Holt, Rinehart and Winston, 1981.
Culler, Jonathan. *The Pursuit of Signs: Semiotics, Literature, Deconstruction*. London and Henley: Routledge, 1981.
— *Structuralist Poetics: Structuralism, Linguistics and the Study of Literature*. London and Henley: Routledge, 1975.
Eagleton, Terry. 'Structuralism and Semiotics', 91–126.
Hawkes, Terence. *Structuralism and Semiotics*. London: Methuen, 1977.
Jameson, Fredric. *The Prison-House of Language: A Critical Account of Structuralism and Russian Formalism*. Princeton, NJ: Princeton University Press, 1972.
Jefferson, Ann. 'Structuralism and Post-Structuralism'. Jefferson and Robey. 84–112.
Kurzweil, Edith. *The Age of Structuralism: Lévi-Strauss to Foucault*. New York: Columbia University Press, 1980.
Scholes, Robert D. *Structuralism in Literature: An Introduction*. New Haven and London: Yale University Press, 1974.
Vance, Eugene. 'Greimas, Freud and the Story of Trouvère Lyric'. Hošek and Parker 93–105.

4
Deconstruction

Deconstruction, properly speaking, is a philosophical, rather than a literary, approach to texts. It is a post-structuralist theory, 'post' here signifying not that deconstruction replaces structuralism as a chronologically more recent theory, but rather that it depends upon structuralism as a prior system of analysis. Developed mainly in France, deconstruction is generally associated with the work of Jacques Derrida, who may be said to have pioneered it as a method of reading texts. Derrida himself, however, acknowledges his own antecedents in the work of philosophers like Kant, Nietzsche, Husserl and Heidegger (whose writing he subjects to searching examination), rather than in the work of earlier literary theorists and critics.

Deconstruction has, since its first appearance, gathered to itself many representatives and defenders, not only in France but also in the United States. In the latter country, it has found a home at Yale University, where it is associated with such names as Geoffrey Hartman, Paul de Man and J. Hillis Miller. Indeed, in the hands of the American critics and theorists, deconstruction has come to be applied more particularly to literary texts, and, in the view of some theorists, has in its American guise (though not specifically that taught at Yale) been assimilated into the still-dominant New Criticism. That is, deconstruction, it is argued, has been domesticated by American academia, and made into a sophisticated, wittier and more idiosyncratic version of the kind of textual reading associated with New Criticism. This, the argument runs, constitutes a betrayal of its origins (a problematic term in deconstructive theory, thus creating a certain irony in this context) as a method of questioning texts of all kinds and our common practices of reading them, in order to show how both the texts and our understanding of them are founded in particular assumptions about language, themselves connected with dominant cultural ideologies.

What is deconstruction? Culler defines it negatively: 'deconstruction is not a theory that defines meaning in order to tell you how to find it'

(Culler, *On Deconstruction* 131). Barbara Johnson calls it 'the careful teasing out of warring forces of signification within the text' (5), while Paul de Man says of the practice of this theory, 'A deconstruction always has for its target to reveal the existence of hidden articulations and fragmentations within assumed monadic totalities' (*Allegories of Reading* 249). For readers reared on literary theories that have as their aim the recognition of a clearly identifiable meaning in the text, both the language of such definitions of this theory, and their statements of its aims, intents or strategies are difficult and confusing. The confusion has not, of course, been diminished by the proliferation in recent years of different 'schools' of deconstructive practice, each often developing its own particular terminology.

One thing emerges clearly from the above definitions, however. Deconstruction is a theory aimed less at producing interpretations of particular texts (though many applications of deconstructive theory to texts have resulted in new, ingenious and sometimes startling interpretations) than at examining how readers read these texts, and how the texts themselves apparently offer *preferred* readings. The 'apparently' of the previous sentence should not be glossed over or taken lightly: deconstruction postulates as a first premiss that the reading of any text is the identification of a particular discourse in it. The process by which we, as readers, arrive at such an identification includes our abilities with the linguistic codes with which we manipulate the meaning of the text; and, because such codes are tied to cultural structures and values, the assumptions and ideologies which we bring to the text, whether these are our own and contemporary, or what we believe to have been the assumptions and ideologies of the culture which produced the text.

Because both language and cultural ideology are larger than the text itself, which must find accommodation in linguistic and cultural codes that may be contradictory, the discourse of the text is unlikely to be unitary and unambiguous. Thus, all texts may be said to contain disruptive elements, points of rupture or gaps which, when perceived and carefully examined, admit other, marginal or non-preferred readings, ones which call into question the apparently obvious, inevitable or familiar meaning found. A deconstructive reading thus searches the text in order to find the points at which the latter's constitutive codes 'undo' themselves.

Our normal practice of reading is to regard language as transparent, as giving directly upon meaning. Structuralist theory, as we have seen, had already questioned this, but in general assumed that the codes of which language is constituted have a stability within the system. Deconstruction interrogates this assumption. For instance, structuralism takes for granted the existence of binary oppositions in the culture and its language: terms like *man/woman, nature/culture, high/low,* according to structuralist theory, assist us in organising reality through language. From the deconstructive viewpoint, however, these are not valueless oppositions: the apparent naturalness by which the first term is chosen in fact implies a hierarchisation or prioritisation, imposed, often unconsciously, upon the opposition. The first term, in other words, is given a positive value, the second a negative. 'Woman', for example, may thus be defined as 'other' to 'man', and therefore — in a culture which has favoured men and male principles — women may be seen as secondary to men. The same argument can be made for *nature/culture,* and, of course, for any other pair of oppositions.

Recognition of this alone, however, is not sufficient. Deconstruction seeks the term by which such oppositions may be, if not reconciled, then at least understood as existing in a relation of tension.[1] One of the ways in which Derrida seeks to do this is in his theory of the *supplement.* This may be defined as a text or element which is added to or is considered secondary to another, more complete textual structure or system. However, as Derrida notes in his discussion of Rousseau, '... *That Dangerous Supplement* ...' (*Of Grammatology* 141–64), if the structure can be added to, it cannot be complete, and if the supplement can be added, it cannot be merely secondary. Thus, if we return to the opposition *nature/culture,* we can see that we commonly think of nature as primary and complete, while culture is secondary, because artificial, and, for the same reason, destined to incompleteness: culture can be considered a supplement to nature. However, by the logic which Derrida articulates his theory of the supplement, nature, despite our post-Romantic attachment to the concept, cannot be complete — it cannot, for instance, be entirely habitable in human terms — otherwise culture would necessarily never have been invented. If culture is not supplementary to nature, we must look for a third term *which includes both 'nature' and 'culture'* .

The same sort of argument can be made for the opposition *man/woman,* which would result, first, in discovering that 'man' has no privileged priority over 'woman', and indeed may even be seen as secondary to 'woman'; and, next, that some other term needs to be sought which sees both 'man' and 'woman' as variants of itself (see Culler's discussion of the implications of deconstructive theory for Freudian psychoanalysis and for feminist theory, *On Deconstruction* 165–75). Central to an understanding of literature, and of poetry in particular, is Derrida's now notorious exploration of the supplemental relation between speech and writing as oppositional terms.

Derrida notes that, even as early as Plato's dialogues, speech as a mode of communication has been privileged over writing. Writing has been seen as a mechanical supplement to speech, which is primary, direct, spontaneous and transparent to meaning. Writing, by contrast, is secondary and more deliberate; it uses rhetorical and literary artifices, so that the thought, meaning or ideas which are to be transferred are in fact mediated through and therefore affected ('contaminated') by writing. This is, of course, the 'commonsense' approach to the relationship between speech and writing with which we are familiar, and is what Derrida describes as *phonocentrism*, or the privileging of the spoken over the written.

However, as Derrida points out, the difficulties and dangers associated with writing are already present in speech. Language being what it is, the pure and uncontaminated expression of one's meaning is an unattainable ideal even in speech, as a little reflection on one's own experience will show. Moreover, language is already permeated with rhetorical figures and tropes,[2] such as metaphor, which is not the property of purely literary texts alone, but occurs frequently even in daily conversational utterances. As de Man observes:

> We know that our entire social language is an intricate system of rhetorical devices designed to escape from the direct expression of desires that are, in the fullest sense of the term, unnameable — not because they are ethically shameful (for this would make the problem a very simple one), but because unmediated expression is a philosophical impossibility. ('Criticism and Crisis', *Blindness and Insight* 9)

These tropes deflect and delay the desired ideal of a direct transfer of intended meaning, regardless of whether one speaks or writes, resulting always in a distortion or doubling of possible meaning. Indeed, given this state of affairs in communication, argues Derrida, it would be more honest to recognise writing as primary, since we accept that it does not attempt to hide the possible and actual slippages of meaning, and the slides from apparently literal to figurative signification which also exist in speech, but which we prefer not to notice.

Such non-recognition is not inevitable. Derrida ascribes it to the *logocentrism* of Western culture. *Logos*, as the *Oxford English Dictionary* informs us, signifies both 'word' and 'reason': thus both the signifier and the intelligence that utters the signifier are bound up in the meaning of this sign. This, Derrida argues, has produced a 'metaphysics of presence' in the thought of Western culture about language. That is, the linguistic utterance has become identified with the presence (real or assumed) of the one who utters. So, when we hear or read a text of any kind, we automatically posit a speaker or writer of that text, no matter how difficult this might prove.[3] Logocentrism, or the metaphysics of presence, is thus the motivating principle behind phonocentrism.

The justification for this iconoclastic rearrangement of the hierarchy which privileges speech over writing is to be found in the myth of origins. We assume that speech came before writing, and that writing was simply a convenient way of transcribing and recording speech. However, Derrida argues that such origins can never be located in reality. We cannot know for sure the historical moment, first, when language originally became articulated in speech, nor, second, when writing first emerged and was differentiated from speech. All we have is hypothesis, based on fragmentary historical evidence, and even this cannot be adduced conclusively. Is the drawing of an animal on a cave wall *the written representation of the word for that animal* in the culture that produced the drawing, or is it *a representation, at the same level as the word, of that animal?*

If writing is indeed a way of reproducing or repeating speech, we must accept that speech itself contains mechanisms by which it can be reproduced and repeated. The downgrading of writing as simply a mode of transcription — of repeating that which is original — is thus a misrepresentation of the nature of speech itself, which is also capable of transcription, from one moment, context or voice to another.

Thus, writing, in which meaning becomes elusive, according to the general cultural myths which oppose writing to speech, truly reflects the real nature of language, since it palpably demonstrates the problems of language itself — that it mediates thought, that it is slippery in meaning, that it uses figurative language which necessarily obscures or distorts ideas (or truths) even as they are conveyed, and so on. Controversially, therefore, and with a certain degree of mischievous playfulness, Derrida advances the notion that writing, as an existent system analogous to the structuralist notion of *langue*, is prior to speech, which is akin to *parole*, the actualisation of that system.[4] This, of course, flies in the face of observed 'fact' and of cultural predisposition.

For Derrida, however, the opposition *speech/writing* disguises what he calls *archi-écriture* or archewriting. Both speech and writing may be seen as manifestations of a third linguistic term, a kind of '(arche)writing', which is in fact a definition of language itself. Here Derrida's own theory comes close to that of Plato, and to the myth of origins, for it is possible to argue that archewriting is simply a version of the Platonic theory of forms, or the ideal essences of things, and thus constitutes a kind of origin for both speech and writing. However, Derrida's notion of archewriting is not that it pre-exists speech and writing, or that these are modelled upon it; rather, his idea is that language operates in a certain fashion, which he labels archewriting, and *that this operation is made visible or manifest in both speech and writing*. Writing, in fact, is to be privileged over speech in that it disguises the function of archewriting less, and discards the myths of presence and immediacy in which speech — for reasons located in cultural ideology and history — has been veiled.

At this point, we may be entitled to ask: given that presence and immediacy of meaning are illusory in both speech and writing, what is meaning itself? Is it, too, illusory? To begin to explore this question, we need to make certain connections between structuralism and deconstruction. In the preceding chapter, we observed that structuralism is an essentially semiotic theory whose claim to mimetic quality rests on its assumption that language is the most important determinant, not only of communication, but of the perception of reality. It is, according to structuralist theory, the first order signifying system. All other systems are modelled upon and depend on it, and are thus second order systems. Thus, structuralism may be defined as a text-oriented theory that foregrounds the process of semiosis; however, if we accept that all perception and communication are grounded in language itself, then that semiotic process can be seen also as a mimetic one, since the language shapes our perceptions and representations of external reality.

As a post-structuralist theory, deconstruction may be described as semiosis in infinite regress. Though structuralism asserts that the connection between language and perceived reality is an arbitrary one and is culturally defined, it does concede or at least imply that the relation between sign and object is stable within the limits of the relevant culture, and within the conspectus of the conscious subjective mind inhabiting that culture. Deconstruction, by contrast, makes no such concession. Meaning in language (and deconstruction accepts the structuralist premiss that language is the first order signifying system) is a question of *différance*, as Derrida puts it. This term is a play on the French meanings of the word. On the one hand, it signifies 'difference', in the same sense that structuralism asserts that signification in language occurs in the interplay of opposition. Deconstruction takes this one step further by arguing that if signs — words — have meaning *only* through difference, 'essential' or 'absolute' meaning does not exist. Rather, what we have is the *trace* of those absent meanings whose differential relationship give meaning to the particular sign before us.

Moreover, this same difference interposes itself between the signifier of the sign and its signified: the physical or material *form* of the sign is marked by its difference from the *meaning* it is supposed to have. As Gayatri Chakravorty Spivak observes in the Translator's Preface to her translation of Derrida's *De la grammatologie*:

Such is the strange 'being' of the sign: half of it always 'not there' and the other half always 'not that'. The structure of the sign is determined by the trace or track of that other which is forever absent. (*Of Grammatology* xvii)

The half that is 'always "not there"' is, of course, the signified — the meaning — to which the sign points, but with which it cannot be identified. The half that is 'always "not that"' is the signifier — the physical or material manifestation of the sign which is essentially worthless without the signifier.

This paradox is intrinsic to language itself, and its consequence is that meaning is always evasive. It is never 'there' where the signifying system is; and the more a text reaches to encase meaning within its structure of signs, the more elusive that meaning becomes. This is the second meaning of *différance*, which in French can mean 'deferral'. Derrida argues that meaning is constantly deferred through the play of signifiers in the language; meaning is always *to be* attained, but never *is* attained.

The philosophical implications of this are large. The traditional stance of Western philosophy, from classical times onwards, has been that it searches for truth. Etymologically, 'philosophy' means 'the love of wisdom or the knowledge of things'. However, since this love of and search for truth can be conducted and articulated only in language, what actually results is a discourse framed in rhetorical structures whose metaphors and other figural tropes may hint referentially at the external and 'real' presence of truth, but which, when examined closely and 'deconstructed', is seen to be a verbal creation or construction of that which philosophy ostensibly seeks to find outside itself.

Derrida's meditations on various key philosophical, historical, critical and psychological texts are therefore directed towards identifying the rhetorical structure in the text which, ironically, allows *both* the *construction* of an apparently present truth, *and its deconstruction*: that is, its exposure as a linguistic structure. This latter is itself highly influenced by preferred cultural myths and ideologies. Thus, Derrida shows that even apparently radical texts — radical, that is, in their time — turn out to be founded on classical, traditional presuppositions. This permits a double deconstruction: in the first place, radicality or innovation turn out to be illusory, and, in the second, the source texts on which the later ones are shown to depend can themselves be identified and deconstructed through intertextual means.

There are two important implications of this position. The first is that deconstruction becomes a constant regression. Not only is the text under consideration to be deconstructed, but also those texts in which it may have its roots. Not only these, but also the essay, book or process by which the deconstruction of the text is effected itself becomes available for deconstruction. This is not, as Derrida sees it, simply a negative process. It is also an enlightening experience, since it exposes certain ideologies and renders them available for examination. It permits an analysis of the relation between language and its structures, and the meaning or signification that these apparently promise. Nor does it privilege the theoretical or critical commentary as itself beyond comment or deconstruction, as many other theories do.

The second implication is that this theory nullifies the traditional distinction between 'creative' or 'literary' writing and others, particularly analytical, critical and other discursive sorts of writing. The distinction depends, first, on the metaphysics of presence, the idea that in literature the writer, in one sense or another, is an actual presence in the text, whereas, in critical writing, the writer hides behind or is parasitic upon the literary text, which is judged as primary. Derrida's thesis of the primacy of all writing reconstructs such texts as located along a spectrum, which exposes all texts to deconstructive scrutiny, regardless of their apparent subjectivity or objectivity.

Second, it depends on what de Man defines, in terms of literature, as 'a language engaged in its highest intent and tending toward the fullest possible self-understanding' ('Form and Intent in the American New Criticism', *Blindness and Insight* 31). By this he means not that the language of literary texts has any greater validity or referentiality than other kinds of language (although he argues that this is how literary texts tend to be read), but that it is conscious of itself as language. Hence:

> The critical interpretation is oriented toward a consciousness which is itself engaged in an act of total interpretation. The relationship between author and critic does not designate a difference in the type of activity involved, since no fundamental discontinuity exists between two acts that both aim at full understanding; the difference is primarily temporal in kind. Poetry is the foreknowledge of criticism. (31)

Derrida's American followers have adopted different aspects of his work, and developed them in particular ways: de Man, for instance, is one of the more rigorous deconstructors in the Derridean vein. He is interested in the way in which the rhetorical structures of a text, particularly its metaphors, apparently construct one kind of meaning, whereas, when subjected to appropriate and rigorous analysis, they can be shown in fact to *de*construct that meaning in favour of another whose ideological implications may be opposed to those actually articulated in the text. Other theoreticians, such as Hartman, have singled out Derrida's notions of language as play, and have developed a theory which extols a carnivalesque enjoyment of puns and games of linguistic and literary association. A useful showcase of these various approaches is to be found in *Deconstruction and Criticism*, which features essays by Harold Bloom, Paul de Man, Jacques Derrida, Geoffrey H. Hartman and J. Hillis Miller.

Before turning to a poetic text, and exploring it from the point of view of deconstructive theory, let us consider, as an example of the technique, the way in which a particular metaphor works in daily usage. We are accustomed, when dealing with financial and economic matters, to employ a certain metaphor which finds various linguistic forms. We speak of 'cash flow', 'cash (or money) liquidity', 'liquidity of assets', and 'liquidation of debts'. The metaphor, evidently, associates fluidity with monetary matters, and a deconstructionist would be interested, first, to know why this metaphor should have become appropriate in this context, and, second, to what this metaphor actually points.

At one level, of course, the metaphor suggests the circulation of cash in the society. However, the most significant transactions in our culture are paper ones, not the actual passing of cash from hand to hand. To speak, therefore, of 'cash flow' or 'liquidity' is to produce the effect of the immediacy of money in a financial structure in which one rarely sees the actual bank bills with which one is dealing. This becomes, in a sense, the economic equivalent of the metaphysics of presence which Derrida detects in much of the philosophical, literary and theoretical writing of our culture.

At another level, the metaphor *naturalises* money, which does not actually flow at all, except when it is metal being minted into coin. (There is an interesting variation of this in film sequences, or in TV commercials, which show coins or bills 'flowing' rapidly past the camera, in order to create the effect of wealth in transit.) Money is thus compared to something familiar, innocuous and innocent, such as water, which is natural and wholesome. In this way, the cultural reprobation of centuries against money and the love of money is disconnected from the fact of money and its circulation in the culture. To love money or to worship Mammon is to adore the actual minted coinage; to enjoy a good cash flow is to support an economy and to benefit society as a whole.

If we consider the metaphor of fluidity a little more closely, though, we can see that the idea of the flow of money or wealth implies its constant presence. When water flows, the stream itself remains present, though the actual molecules of water themselves disappear continually and forever from view. This paradoxical state of affairs was already understood by Heraclitus in the sixth century BC. His theory that the universe is in flux found expression in a number of metaphorical statements which often used the image of flowing water, including what is probably his best-known observation: 'You cannot step twice into the same river; for fresh waters are ever flowing in upon you.'[5] The financial metaphor is an invitation to see economic transactions in the same light, even though our individual experience might suggest that money actually vanishes faster than it is replenished.

It is, therefore, ironical that the same metaphor should be invoked when we wish to talk about a cash non-flow, as in 'liquidation of debts'. A debt implies an interruption in the circulation of money, and an interruption of this kind cannot simply be rendered fluid: that is, a debt cannot be circulated in quite the same way as cash can, although, of course, economists and merchants are highly sensitive to the effect of debt on the economy and on trade. Moreover, what becomes emphasised in this particular use of the metaphor is precisely the fact that money is not magically and naturally replenished in its flow, as a stream of water is. Thus, the metaphor is used both positively to signify the circulation of money, and negatively to signify an interruption in its circulation, and the consequent need to mend this break in the economic structure. This contradiction produces an *aporia*, a rhetorical term meaning a paradox or ambiguity which prevents us from knowing which sense is the appropriate one. Thus, the deconstructive reflection on the way in which language works shows the latter to be suffused, on the one hand, with implicit ideologies that direct our way of thinking, and, on the other, riddled with gaps which create discontinuities in the process of meaning itself.

An important point to note in this connection, however, is that, according to Derrida and others, such discontinuities, contradictions and paradoxes are embedded in the structure of language itself: we cannot rid ourselves of them without ridding ourselves entirely of our mode of communication. Rather, we should sensitise ourselves to these elements of language, which function as background to our daily communication, and learn to read all kinds of texts, whether spoken, written or visual, discursive or fictional, with the awareness that they are shot through with contradictions and with unarticulated premises that dictate how we are to understand them.

Of course, when we turn our attention away from a particular metaphor to a poetic text which is constructed of many kinds of rhetorical figures and tropes, we encounter a much more complex system of overt and covert ideological directives. To conduct a complete deconstruction of such a text requires not only that the poem itself first be read, and then deconstructed in terms of its verbal structure, but also that its philosophical or ideological statements be traced back to their sources and tested. Such a deconstruction is clearly beyond the scope of the present exercise; instead, we will limit ourselves to examining how the verbal structure of the poetic text may be deconstructed, and to setting the text's philosophical content within a general historical and cultural context only.

Deconstruction in Practice

Design

I found a dimpled spider, fat and white,
On a white heal-all, holding up a moth
Like a white piece of rigid satin cloth —
Assorted characters of death and blight
Mixed ready to begin the morning right,
Like the ingredients of a witches' broth —
A snow-drop spider, a flower like froth,
And dead wings carried like a paper kite.

What had that flower to do with being white,
The wayside blue and innocent heal-all?
What brought the kindred spider to that height,
Then steered the white moth thither in the night?
What but design of darkness to appall? —
If design govern in a thing so small.

Robert Frost

On the face of it, this sonnet seems to be fairly straightforward. The speaker describes an unusual event which he has witnessed, a white spider on a white heal-all (a plant which normally has blue flowers), devouring a white moth. The speaker then goes on to inquire whether this conjunction of white-on-white-on-white is coincidental or intentional, and what this might mean in terms of the structure of reality. However, the title of the poem, 'Design', should alert us to a potential series of contradictions or paradoxes. A design may be defined as the arrangement of elements in a pleasing and/or useful configuration: such a definition would certainly cover the white-on-white-on-white features in the poem, and their usefulness, at least as seen from the spider's point of view. However, a design may also be an intent, a plan to manipulate others to one's own advantage. This is the question asked towards the end of the poem: to whose advantage has been this particular arrangement or rearrangement of elements?

From the perspective of the deconstructor reading the text, these two definitions are in effect opposed. One — the first — implies a passivity in the notion of design: the elements are made to correspond to an abstract arrangement, and are moved by an unknown, and finally unidentified, force or agency. The emphasis, in this definition, however, is on the actual physical constellation of the elements: the design as seen by an onlooker. The second definition, on the other hand, implies activity, in that implicit in it or postulated by it is the presence of a designing mind. This may be benign or malign in its intents, though the usual association with this definition is malignity, at worst, and selfishness, at best, whereas 'design', in its first definition, remains relatively neutral.

We are thus confronted with a concept of design that is not simply ambiguous, but contradictory. It is both passive and active, both overt and covert (one design can be seen, the other only guessed at), both neutral and charged with (generally negative) associations. In all such oppositions, deconstructionist theory warns us, the first term is generally given priority because of the assumptions embedded in the culture. Thus, as we consider these two definitions implied by 'design', we are likely to prefer the first over the second, because the myths and morality of our culture compel us to ally with passivity (this may be seen in the Christian ideal of patience, which etymologically means 'suffering'); with overt intention (hence the emphasis in our culture on confession, including Christian confession, such articulations of intent as declarations of war, and Freudian psychoanalysis); and with neutrality (exemplified in our myths surrounding the concepts of justice, rational argument, and so on). It is not hard, however, to imagine a culture in which an individual would not survive to anything like a ripe old age if he or she persisted in upholding these particular ideals: for example, Imperial Rome under Nero or Caligula must have created a climate hostile to such principles. So these ideals are not 'natural': they are privileged by our culture.

There is a third sense of 'design', however, which we might wish to consider as an 'archedesign'. The two other significations may be characterised as 'design in (a particular medium)' and 'design by or for (a particular subject or personage)'. The 'archedesign' may be thought of as 'design upon (a particular object or victim)'. There is, of course, a victim in the poem's little story: the moth, for whose demise everything else seems to have been arranged. However, there is another, less obvious victim in this 'design' of the poem, namely, the reader.

At first sight this may seem a little far-fetched. The reader, surely, is simply the recipient of the text: the reader's task is merely making sense of its content. However, attention paid to the strategies of the poem, and to the kind of discourse which it offers will show that the reader's participation in the poem is neither neutral nor innocent.

Let us begin by considering, first, the fact that this poem is a sonnet. We might characterise the sonnet form as one that is quintessentially 'designed', requiring, as it does (at least in its traditional forms, and 'Design' belongs to these), certain elements, such as an octave and a sestet, a 'turn' of thought at the end of the octave, and (especially in the English sonnet) a pithy conclusion, with its suggestion of a universal truth. Thus, the reader is primed, upon recognising the poem to be a sonnet, to expect certain features to occur — and they do, with the exception of the universalising statement of truth at the poem's conclusion. Frost's poem seems to withdraw from any such positive statement.

Second, the aesthetic or functional design described in the poem is one which allows the relationships of white-to-white-to-white to be questioned. The poem thus invites us to invoke the usual cultural associations of the colour white, such as innocence and purity, and to reassess them in terms of their configuration in the poem's narrative. Is the heal-all simply a neutral or innocent setting for the spider's carnivorous appetite? If so, why is the flower white, when it is normally blue? Is the spider simply a natural creature indulging its natural appetite? If so, why is it albino in colouring, and located in a white flower? And so on: the questions implicit in the text may be articulated and multiplied further, and they will tend towards asking whether white is not metaphorically or symbolically black, and whether the cover associations of innocence, neutrality or purity do not simply mask a malign and impure motivation or agency. However, if we consider the poem to be also a design upon the reader, we might notice that it is more obviously, in terms of the text printed on the page, a design in black upon white, a relationship which inverts the one suggested in the poem, but which is hinted at in the development of the poem's argument.

Third, we might wish to consider the relationship of the octave to the sestet in this particular poem. In the octave, we are told a story which is ostensibly the experience of the speaking subject of the text. In the sestet, the speaker asks a series of questions which culminate in the climactic query as to whether it is evil which organises events in our world. The final line retreats a little from this position, finding expression in a question framed as a statement: 'If design govern in a thing so small.' This disguised question (Does design govern in small things?) has no real or satisfying answer. To respond to it in the affirmative is to accept that everything including all events in one's life have been mapped out by some superior force at some prior time, and that therefore we have no free will or decision-making power of our own. Ours is simply to act out the script written for us and without our knowledge. To answer in the negative, on the other hand, is to align oneself with the view that there is no organisation in the universe, and that all events are simply random happenings. The consequence of this is that nothing we do or achieve can have any value or meaning in the larger order of things, because there *is* no larger order.

The logic of the poem's closing rhetorical strategy is thus to create a pair of contradictory antitheses: to deny the proposition of the last line is both to affirm free will and to accept a consequent chaos. To affirm it is to deny free will, and to accept tyrannical order. The poem leads us, therefore, to a logical and rhetorical *aporia*, on the one hand, and, on the other, to a moral dilemma, since our culture prompts us to assume *both* free will *and* guidance from above (whether defined as God's will or the operation of some other mysterious, impersonal force), often without our being aware of the internal contradiction that this poses.

This dilemma emerges from the particular kind of discourse of the text. The poem apparently presents in a neutral way a particular observation or experience of reality. However, the terms by which its details transmitted to us are already suffused with ambiguity. For example, the 'dimpled spider' of the first line might suggest simultaneously, on the one hand, innocence and charm (we value dimples in our culture for these qualities), and predatory patience and voraciousness, on the other. Similarly, the adjoining description of the spider as 'fat and white' suggests both well-being ('fat') and ill-health ('white'), producing the effect of a repellent obesity. This pair of contradictory meanings combines with the earlier one to create a grotesque image of charm and ugliness, innocence and predatoriness, health and ill-health.

Similar contradictions can be found in the two other protagonists of the little drama described by the speaker. The normally blue heal-all, whose name alone suggests that it is a plant of some virtue, is itself blanched and rendered 'unnatural' or diseased; while the moth, rigid in death, is described both as a 'piece of satin cloth' — that is, awaiting its transformation into some shape — and as a 'paper kite', a finished product, made of less fancy material than satin. The idea of trans-formation is present also in the poem in a theological sense, for the chalice in the sacrament of Communion is generally also covered with white satin cloth. However, whereas the wafer and the wine are magically transformed into the body and blood of Christ through the mystery of the Communion, in this 'morning [mourning] right [rite]' the living moth is literally converted into dead matter awaiting consumption by the spider, whose role now modulates into that of officiating priest.

And what kind of rite is it that this priest performs? The text suggests that it is a ritual of black magic, for these elements are 'Like the ingredients of a witches' broth.' Here again a dubious meaning interposes itself. We know, from examples like Shakespeare's *Macbeth*, that a witches' broth is not likely to be wholesome, and that its purpose is probably malign. On the other hand, the folk wisdom of

our culture tells us that a *broth* (which is a thin soup in which meat
has been boiled) is in fact extremely nourishing, especially in cases of
illness. How, then, are we to understand line 6: is this apparent
witches' broth an evil concoction, or a medicinal decoction?

The problem has already been posed earlier in the poem, where we
are told that the three protagonists are 'Assorted characters of death
and blight/ Mixed ready to begin the morning right.' 'Character' may
signify a part in a play, in which case the figures described are make-
believe, illusory, not authentic. Or the word may signify something
like 'personality', in which case connected not simply with a spider, a
plant and a moth, but with a cunning and malevolent spider, an ailing
and feeble heal-all, and a victimised and dead moth — truly 'Assorted
characters of death and blight.' The third sense of 'character' is one to
which we shall return: in this signification, 'character' means something like 'marks', as on a page, just as the letters of the alphabet are
characters. In this sense, this assortment of characters *spells out* 'death
and blight': this is the 'meaning', as it were, of the event described.
Given these three kinds of signification for the word, the assortment
of characters is appropriate for a witches' broth, containing as it does
malignancy (the spider), disease (the heal-all), and innocence annihi-
lated (the unsuspecting moth trapped and seized by the spider),
together with the suggestion of a spell.

The second line develops the ambiguity further. These elements
are 'Mixed ready to begin the morning right', the formulation of
this idea sounding rather like a commercial jingle for a breakfast
cereal. However, as we saw above, 'morning' is a homonym of
'mourning', and 'right' of 'rite'. This line transforms the ritual of
breakfast, a morning meal, into something more alien and frightening:
both a morning meal which occurs when one is awake, and a wake
which occurs when one is mourning.

Throughout the octave, then, Frost is concerned to establish
several possible meanings which operate concurrently, and which
conflict with, or act as comments upon, one another. However, where
a New Critical reading might regard these multiple meanings as
stabilised within an ironic structure which encourages ambiguity, the
deconstructive reading sees them as duplicitous: they are 'designed' to
lead the reader in two, mutually incompatible directions, as the closing lines of the sonnet make clear.[6] It is here that we may see in
operation Derrida's notion of *différance*, for each of the double meanings is in fact defined by the other or others, so that even a line so
ostensibly simple and intelligible as 'I saw a dimpled spider, fat and
white' offers only traces of meaning, the evidence of significations
which *are not* actually present, but which, given the systemic nature
of language, *have been* present. This is demonstrated more clearly

by Frost's use of 'appall', whose sense appears to be situated as a trace between the meanings 'to dismay' and 'to cause to go pale or dim', and between these and to cover with a pall (a covering often of black or white velvet or other fine cloth). There is no 'right' meaning for the word, since all three are arguably validated by the context of the poem, yet the assumption of one may preclude the presence of the others.

Underlying the duplicity of the text is a particular activity which is signalled to us by line 4, and it is here we return to the third meaning of 'characters', that is, marks or signs on a page. Frost draws our attention to these lines by placing them at the centre of the octave. Though they are, respectively, the last line of the first quatrain and the first of the second quatrain, Frost's retention of the traditional rhyme scheme of the English sonnet allows lines 4 and 5 to rhyme together. Their correspondent rhymes, according to this scheme, fall in lines 1 and 8 of the octave: the distance thus created isolates lines 4 and 5, which are further emphasised by being offset as a parenthesis to the description developed in this part of the poem. The parenthesis is actually completed in line 6, and is marked by the presence of a pair of dashes at the end of lines 3 and 6.

We are thus encouraged to pay more attention to this group of lines than its apparent status as parenthesis might otherwise warrant. This causes us to focus, therefore, on the different significations of 'Assorted characters'. The first two senses — those of 'characters in a play' and 'personalities' — are clearly related to the 'plot' of the story being told in the poem; the third, however, though also connected to the same 'plot', in addition alerts us to the nature of the poem itself. It, too, is composed of 'Assorted characters of death and blight', or rather it is Frost's particular way of assorting his characters — choosing and combining the words — that produces his tale of death and blight.

Moreover, Frost capitalises on the reader's inclination to invoke a metaphysics of presence, and to assume not only that there is a speaker who utters the lines of the poem, but also that this speaker probably knows the answer to the question implicit in the final line. This strategy apparently confirms for us the principle of a truth that is absolute and external to ourselves, even though we may not be privileged to perceive (or receive) it. Yet this wise speaker is produced *by the text and its rhetoric*, and the fear and suspicion provoked by the poem's theme is the more enhanced by our feeling that information — truth — is being withheld from us by the speaker, a feeling which the text works hard to create and sustain.

The story that the poem tells us, then, does not bear any particular relation to reality, or to an actual experience of the poet himself. A verbal construct, the text deliberately exploits the ambiguity inherent in language. The opening phrase, 'I found ...' appears to refer to a real, prior event; however, the account given turns out to be in fact an assortment of characters — or signs — whose purpose is to lead the reader to answer an unanswerable question, to make a choice that is not really a choice. Moreover, the strategy of the text is to ask questions in a sestet that confirms for us our assumption of the presence of an actual speaking subject, one who is capable of recounting an experience and then reflecting on it. The poem's conclusion, however, is an imposition upon the reader both of that experience and its attendant questions, and a demand that readers provide an authentic and considered response to an important question which turns out, in fact, to be simply the product of a series of rhetorical and strategic manoeuvres of the text.

That this is so may be seen in the way that it constructs out of what may once have been an actual event, a fiction, if by this we understand a text aware of itself as a text. For how else may we define this tale of the spider, the heal-all and the moth, with its recurrent emphasis on the colour white, on the ambiguity of this colour and on the duplicities of meaning in the signs actually used to recount the tale to us? Such formal definition and such manipulation of the reader's response to the text go beyond a merely neutral account of an event observed. Moreover, these strategies point up the impossibility of pure referentiality in language, since to frame such events in a sequential account of any kind is to make selections and choices that automatically fictionalise or distort the actual experience.

Further evidence of the rhetorical strategies deployed in the poem may be seen in the relation of octave to sestet. In our consideration of 'Design' so far, we have nominated the octave as recounting a 'story' of sorts, and the sestet as commenting on that story by asking a series of questions. The structural relationship, then, appears to be that of cause to effect: the events of the octave lead to the questions of the sestet. However, if we isolate those questions, we will see that they are reducible to a single interrogative: why does X happen to A? Once understood in this form, the questions turn out to be variants of questions about the human condition. Similar inquiries have, since ancient times, resulted, on the one hand, in philosophical and theological speculations on such themes as 'Why are we here?', 'Why do we suffer?', 'Is there a benevolent deity who watches over us?' or 'Why do we die?' They are unanswerable questions: reasoning them out leads, finally, to a rupture in the line of argument that can be patched over only by faith, which is antithetical, if not hostile, to reason. This is as true of Socrates' philosophical theory of the soul's existence after death, in Plato's *Phaedo*, as it is of Descartes' attempt in the seventeenth century to prove the existence of God mathematically in the

Discourse of Method, as well as of subsequent arguments and 'proofs' since the Cartesian inauguration of the age of science and reason.

On the other hand, the question 'Why does X happen to A?' also produces the kind of enquiry which we label 'scientific', that is, which may arrive at some answer through observation, experiment or other empirical means. However, as we have already noted, the apparently neutral observation of events presented in the octave turns out, instead, to be a fiction. Whether or not this account is derived from real experience is, as we have seen, finally irrelevant to the actual presentation of the account. Nevertheless, part of the poem's strategy is to present itself as objective, neutral and 'scientific', and then to ask questions which are subjective, partial and not susceptible to scientific argument or proof.

Seen in this light, it appears that the questions which provide the focus for the sestet in Frost's poem are not generated by the events described in the octave. Rather, they are common to the ruminations of the culture as a whole upon its own origins and to its reflections upon its own end (in the senses both of 'conclusion' and 'goal'). As 'insights' into the nature of the events of the poem's story, they are worthless, for in a special sense they generate the story as a convenient fiction, a reason for posing these already existing questions. Cause and effect are reversed in 'Design', so that the tail wags the dog. The poem is thus converted into a kind of palindrome, that troping or design upon language which allows a word or sequence of words to read the same forwards and backwards. Thus the normal linear, serial development of signification is subverted, and language recoils upon itself. In the case of Frost's poem, we are confronted with a text which, read in one direction (from the octave to sestet), asks of a fictionalised situation questions to which there are no answers, and, in another (from the sestet to the octave), offers merely an instance in which such questions might be asked.[7]

Notes

1.   Indeed, deconstructive theory is wary of attempts to effect a reconciliation between oppositions, or to find a position of stability between them. The terms of their relations are founded on tension and instability, and to attempt to smooth over these characteristics, or to elide them, would be to privilege one of the elements of the opposition and then to pretend, even if unknowingly, that this is not the case.

2.   Trope: 'A figure of speech which consists in the use of a word or phrase in a sense other than that which is proper to it' (*OED*).

3.   It is interesting to note in this connection the New Critical insistence that the text of a poem is uttered by someone to someone else, in a particular (dramatic) context: here is an example of the metaphysics of presence clearly articulated in a practice of reading poetry.

4. Saussure distinguished between *langue* as the linguistic system, and *parole* as actual linguistic utterance.
5. Cited in Bertrand Russell, *History of Western Philosophy and its Connection with Political and Social Circumstances from the Earliest Times to the Present Day*. 2nd edn. (London: Allen & Unwin, 1961) 63.
6. De Man comments on the difficulties experienced by New Criticism in simultaneously asserting the organic unity of the literary text and isolating in it conflicting and ambiguous significations:

    > American criticism does not discover a single meaning, but a plurality of ... significations that can be radically opposed to each other. Instead of revealing a continuity affiliated with the coherence of the natural world, it takes us into a discontinuous world of reflective irony and ambiguity. Almost in spite of itself, it pushes the interpretative process so far that the analogy between the organic world and the language of poetry finally explodes. This unitarian criticism finally becomes a criticism of ambiguity, an ironic reflection on the absence of unity it had postulated. ('Form and Intent in the American New Criticism', *Blindness and Insight* 28).

7. A more extended deconstruction of Frost's poem would explore, among other issues, the way in which 'Design' itself deconstructs the traditional sonnet form. In the early Italian and English models, the tight organisation of the sonnet presents, in the octave, a situation, and, in the sestet, a development of, or a reversal in, that situation, leading to a perception, couched typically as a summary of the situation, an insight into it, or — especially in the English sonnet — a generalising apophthegm, a concise and witty proverbial saying or maxim. The sonnet may thus be seen as participating in and representing a particular and familiar epistemology (theory of the nature of knowledge, and hence also a way of knowing), namely, the selective use of experience and incident to deduce something about the nature and dynamics of the universe at large. Our reading of Frost's 'Design' shows that the poem's refusal to provide such a conclusion exposes, first, the fictionality — the constructedness — of the poem's own use of incident, and, second, the artifice of the sonnet as an epistemological strategy. This in turn raises questions about the history and nature of epistemology in the culture as a whole, and the procedures by which knowledge is attained.

Suggestions for Further Reading

Primary

Abrams, M.H. 'The Deconstructive Angel'. Lodge, *Modern Criticism* 265–76.
Bloom, Harold, Paul de Man, *et al. Deconstruction and Criticism*. London and Henley: Routledge, 1979.
Culler, Jonathan. *On Deconstruction: Theory and Criticism After Structuralism*. London, Melbourne and Henley: Routledge, 1983.
— *The Pursuit of Signs: Semiotics, Literature, Deconstruction*. London and

Henley: Routledge, 1981.

De Man, Paul. *Allegories of Reading: Figural Language in Rousseau, Nietzsche, Rilke, and Proust.* New Haven and London: Yale University Press, 1979.

— *Blindness and Insight: Essays in the Rhetoric of Contemporary Criticism.* London: Methuen, 1983.

— 'The Resistance to Theory'. Lodge, *Modern Criticism* 355–71.

Derrida, Jacques. *Dissemination.* Trans. Barbara Johnson. Chicago: University of Chicago Press, 1981.

— *Of Grammatology.* Trans. Gayatri Chakravorty Spivak. Baltimore and London: Johns Hopkins University Press, 1976.

— 'Structure, Sign and Play in the Discourse of the Human Sciences'. Lodge, *Modern Criticism* 108–23.

— *Writing and Difference.* Trans. Alan Bass. London and Henley: Routledge, 1978.

Johnson, Barbara. *The Critical Difference: Essays in the Contemporary Rhetoric of Reading.* Baltimore and London: Johns Hopkins University Press, 1980.

Miller, J. Hillis. 'The Critic as Host'. Lodge, *Modern Criticism* 278–85.

Secondary

Abrams, M.H. 'Deconstruction'. *A Glossary of Literary Terms.* 4th edn. New York: Holt, Rinehart & Winston, 1981.

Arac, Jonathan, Wlad Godzich and Wallace Martin, eds. *The Yale Critics: Deconstruction in America.* Theory and History of Literature, Volume 6. Minneapolis: University of Minnesota Press, 1983.

Culler, Jonathan. 'Jacques Derrida'. Sturrock 154–80.

Eagleton, Terry. 'Post-Structuralism'. 127–50.

Jefferson, Ann. 'Structuralism and Post-Structuralism'. Jefferson and Robey 84–112.

Norris, Christopher. *Deconstruction: Theory and Practice.* London and New York: Methuen, 1982.

— *Derrida.* London: Fontana, 1987.

Ray, William. 'Paul de Man: The Irony of Deconstruction/ The Deconstruction of Irony'. *Literary Meaning: From Phenomenology to Deconstruction.* Oxford: Blackwell, 1984. 186–205.

5

Russian Formalism

In the remaining chapters, we shall be looking at theoretical approaches concerned principally with the integration of literature and the individual literary text into a larger view. Though these often deliver readings of particular texts, their meaning is subordinated to the larger view in that the reading is seen principally as an example or illustration of the theoretical viewpoint. In the case of Russian Formalism, the viewpoint in question is the poetics of the literary text.

Russian Formalism, also variously known as Russian or Soviet poetics, semiotics or structuralism, has certain striking affinities with, and similarities to, both Anglo-American New Criticism and French (Saussurean) structuralism. It emerged during World War I, and thus was approximately contemporaneous with the early phase of New Criticism and Saussurean linguistics. Its theorists, however, remained in large part unaware of the formalism of New Criticism (as, indeed, the New Critics were of developments in Russian literary theory), though both schools of theory proceeded in part from similar philosophical antecedents in the late nineteenth century.

The resemblance of Russian Formalism to structuralism is explained by the fact that Saussure's theory exercised an influence on early Formalist thought — especially that of the linguist Roman Jakobson, — through the work of Sergei Karchevsky, a student of Saussure (Steiner 208).[1] French theory was itself powerfully influenced by Russian Formalism and its offshoot, Prague Structuralism. Indeed, the very term structuralism, as we noted in Chapter 3, was coined by Roman Jakobson, a member both of the Formalist group in Moscow, and later also of the Prague Linguistic Circle.

Readers coming for the first time to key Formalist texts may be struck by certain features. The first of these is the profusion of points of view and methodologies of reading, as well as the argumentative nature of the various articles, essays and books. Formalism misleadingly suggests a certain unanimity of approach, namely, an attention paid exclusively to the form rather than the content of the literary text. However, it should be understood from the outset that the designation Formalist was not one that the group so named chose for themselves: it was imposed upon them by theorists and critics hostile to their work and to its implications. Later, the group defiantly accepted the soubriquet Formalist as a sort of challenge to their opponents.

The heterogeneity of approach within Formalist theory may be explained, at least in part, by the heterogeneity of the group itself. This body of theorists, historians, linguists and critics was in fact constituted by two main groups, each with different theoretical leanings and different objectives. The Moscow Linguistic Circle was formed in 1915 by a group of students at Moscow University, and led by Roman Jakobson. It included Piotr Bogatyrev (later a distinguished Slavic folklorist), Vladimir Propp (also a folklorist), Grigori Vinokur (a linguist), Osip Brik and Boris Tomashevsky, (literary theorists and historians).

The *Opoyaz*[2] group, established in 1916, was based in St Petersburg and, according to Victor Erlich, was itself made up of two sub-groups with differing interests:

> The Society for the Study of Poetic Language or *Opojaz* was a somewhat more heterogeneous team than its Moscow counterpart. The latter represented the linguists' collective venture into poetics. The former was a 'coalition' of two distinct groups: the professional students of language of Baudouin de Courtenay's school ... and literary theoreticians ... who attempted to solve the problems of their discipline by making use of modern linguistics. (*Russian Formalism* 66)

This aggregation of skills and talents was led by the brilliant, iconoclastic and somewhat erratic Victor Shklovsky, (considered by many to be the founder of the Formalist movement), and included Lev Jakubinsky (a linguist) and Boris Eikhenbaum (a literary theorist and historian).

The Formalists attracted members of various theoretical and ideological stripes. Mikhail Bakhtin, for instance, was for a while on the fringes of the Moscow group, but finally repudiated his association with the Formalists on the basis of his political affiliation and his different approach to literature.[3] Others — Boris Tomashevsky is an instance here — were somewhat older than the average age of the group, and brought with them a more traditional scholarship. The important point, however, is that the Formalists did not consider themselves a monolithic, homogeneous whole: they argued not only with members of other schools, traditions or ideologies, but also amongst themselves. Formalism was conceived as a sort of continuous dialogue, developing itself out of debate, question and challenge. Peter Steiner remarks:

> What characterizes Formalism ... is its 'eristic' mode of theorizing: its refusal to reduce the heterogeneity of art to a single explanatory scheme. 'Enough of monism!' Èjchenbaum had declared in 1922. 'We are pluralists. Life is diverse and cannot be reduced to a single principle.' By proceeding from very dissimilar premises, the young scholars turned their presuppositions against themselves, under-cutting, subverting, and refuting each other. (259)

For this reason, Formalism cannot be reduced to a simple statement of principles and methodology. In its very polemicism, Formalism maintained an exciting and dynamic responsiveness to art, to litera-ture and to writing and theorising about these. The liquidation of the group around 1930 meant that many of the theses and ideas of its members had not yet been fully worked out, though, as Èikhenbaum remarks in his 1925 assessment of the already beleaguered movement and its evolution:

> We have no theory that can be laid out as a fixed, ready-made system. For us theory and history merge not only in words, but in fact. We are too well trained by history itself to think that it can be avoided. When we feel that we have a theory that explains every-thing, a ready-made theory explaining all past and future events and therefore needing neither evolution nor anything like it — then we must recognize that the formal method has come to an end, that the spirit of scientific investigation has departed from it. As yet, that has not happened. ('The Theory of the "Formal Method"' 139)

The history of the movement may be divided into two periods or phases, approximately 1915–20, and 1921–30. The earlier period was energised by the work of Victor Shklovsky, who provided some of the central concepts and terminology of the theory. The *Opoyaz* group's work, as Erlich notes, was focused on questions of poetic language and phonetics, though members of *Opoyaz* also made important con-tributions to the study of narrative (74). Indeed, after 1920 theoretical explorations in narrative preoccupied the members of *Opoyaz* more and more (Erlich 87).

The *Opoyaz* theorists in this group were interested in the difference between 'practical' speech and poetic language, seeing in the second a heightening of attention to the actual *sounds* of language, and a con-scious manipulation of various schemes or devices, such as repetitions of sounds or of sound patterns, whereas in practical speech, content over-rides formal qualities, so that language itself becomes merely a vehicle for concept. (This same notion emerges in Roman Jakobson's bipartite model of the factors and functions of language: he distinguishes, as we saw in the chapter on structuralism, between the *referential* or practical function of language, and the *poetic* or self-referential function.)

After 1920, Formalism 'had not only attracted wide notice in the critical reviews, but also established powerful bases of operation in academic literary scholarship. One such position became the "Division of Literary History" formed at the Petrograd State Institute of Art History, in 1920' (Erlich 85). This later phase of Formalist theory also saw the diffusion of the theoretical principles into wider areas of interest, including poetry, drama and theatre, film, folk tales and customs, and so on. It was also in this later phase of development that differences between the Petersburg and Moscow groups grew in intensity.

> The main bone of contention was the problem of the mutual relationship between literary scholarship and linguistics ... The *Opojaz* chieftains were primarily literary historians who turned to linguistics for a viable set of conceptual tools needed in grappling with problems of literary theory. The Muscovites, on the contrary, were predominantly students of language, who found in modern poetry a testing ground for their methodological assumptions. (Erlich 94)

During this period also, Formalism spread from the Soviet Union westward, principally to Czechoslovakia, but also to Poland. Roman Jakobson left Moscow in 1920 to become a founder-member of the Prague Linguistic Circle, whose very name echoes that of the Moscow Linguistic Circle.[4] He invited Formalist colleagues such as Tomashevsky and Tynyanov to visit Prague and read papers to the members of this outgrowth of Russian Formalism. From Czechoslovakia and Poland, situated on the margin between the Soviet bloc and the West, the theory or, rather, theories of Russian Formalism spread elsewhere in Europe, particularly after World War II. Indeed, for some time in the West, Formalist principles were known chiefly in their guise as French structuralism through the work of figures like Claude Lévi-Strauss and Roland Barthes. As we saw in Chapter 3, Lévi-Strauss encountered structuralism through his contact with the erstwhile Formalist Jakobson in New York. Tzvetan Todorov's translations into French in the early 1960s of several key Formalist works proved influential on the writing of Barthes and others.

Initially, Victor Shklovsky and his colleagues sought to discover the nature of 'literariness' (*literaturnost*) by analysing structures of *meaning*. The literary text was thus seen to be a semiotic structure rather than a mimetic representation of reality or a reflection of cultural preoccupations with history, sociology, biography, psychology, politics and so on. The latter were not regarded as intrinsically *literary* in nature; the structure of the literary work was. In order to investigate further, Shklovsky used several strategies.

One of these was to oppose the current and common view that the function of art is to represent life. He distinguished between art, on the one hand, and, on the other, reality, or everyday events and objects (which he called *byt*, an untranslatable Russian term). The work of art, he argued, represents not reality, but art itself, or, more properly, artfulness. It uses *byt* for its raw material, but in selecting, organising and presenting that reality, art ceases to reflect it, and instead becomes a matter of technique, deploying devices, strategies and methods of representation. In other words, the work of art is entirely intertextual with other such works, and bypasses reality and history entirely.

However, the strategies which art employs eventually become familiar to the extent that we fail to recognise them any longer as art. Shklovsky relates this to our general experience:

> If we start to examine the general laws of perception, we see that as perception becomes habitual, it becomes automatic. Thus, for example, all of our habits retreat into the area of the unconsciously automatic; if one remembers the sensations of holding a pen or of speaking in a foreign language for the first time and compares that with his feeling at performing the action for the ten thousandth time, he will agree with us... By this 'algebraic' method of thought we apprehend objects only as shapes with imprecise extensions; we do not see them in their entirety but rather recognize them by their main characteristics. We see the object as though it were enveloped in a sack. We know what it is by its configuration, but we see only its silhouette. ('Art as Technique' 11)

The proper function of art is to 'roughen' that perception, to impede the viewer's processing of the work of art, and to cause the viewer to focus more sharply on the work, in order to perceive more clearly the devices and strategies that it employs.

It is for this reason that Shklovsky unexpectedly, and with some mischief, hails Laurence Sterne's *Tristram Shandy* as 'the most typical novel in world literature'.[5] In Shklovsky's view, Sterne draws the reader's attention continually to devices of narration, to conventions of narrative, in short, to a consciousness of the literary work as a bundle of strategies, rather than as a representation of a reality of any kind. Because it is so open and obvious in its laying bare of its devices, Sterne's novel, in Shklovsky's view, is an epitome of all works of art.[6]

Their task is to estrange us as viewer/readers, and to cause us to perceive the individual work in a new light, aware of the techniques involved in their production. Shklovsky pushes this function of the work of art a step further, however:

> The process of 'algebrization', the over-automatization of an object, permits the greatest economy of perceptive effort. Either objects are assigned only one proper feature — a number, for example — or else they function as though by formula and do not even appear in cognition ...
>
> And so life is reckoned as nothing. Habitualization devours works, clothes, furniture, one's wife, and the fear of war. 'If the whole complex lives of many people go on unconsciously, then such lives are as if they had never been.' And art exists that one may recover the sensation of life; it exists to make one feel things, to make the stone *stony*. The purpose of art is to impart the sensation of things as they are perceived and not as they are known. The technique of art is to make objects 'unfamiliar', to make forms difficult, to increase the difficulty and length of perception because the process of perception is an aesthetic end in itself and must be prolonged. *Art is a way of experiencing the artfulness of an object; the object is not important.* (12; Shklovsky's italics)

What is interesting about this passage is that Shklovsky wants to argue two contradictory views. On the one hand, as we have just seen, he wishes to stress that the function of art is self-directed, not reality-oriented: the artfulness of (representing) an object is more important than the object itself. On the other, he argues also that art causes us to experience — perceive — life or reality more acutely also. This has certain implications for his premiss that art is self-contained and has no reference to reality, except as a source of raw material.

Nonetheless, the notion of the device as the primary element in the literary work became important in Formalist theory. In identifying the devices employed in the text, the reader also discovers how a dominant device *deforms* the others and subordinates them. Boris Eikhenbaum was the first to explore this notion, but it quickly became current among other Formalists:

> [Eikhenbaum] saw the work not as a harmonious correlation of parts and wholes but as a dialectic tension among them. 'The work of art', Èjchenbaum argued, 'is always the result of a complex struggle among various form-creating elements; it is always a kind of compromise. These elements do not simply coexist and "correlate". Depending on the general character of the style, this or that

element acquires the role of the organizing dominant governing all the others and subordinating them to its needs.' (Steiner 105)

Jakobson also espoused this notion: the dominant, he remarks, 'may be defined as the focusing component of a work of art: it rules, determines, and transforms the remaining components. It is the dominant which guarantees the integrity of the structure' ('The Dominant', Matejka and Pomorska 82). However, he expands the notion of the dominant to include the idea of historical development, something which the early work of the Formalists had tended to avoid. Jakobson observes that a dominant may function 'not only in the poetic work of an individual artist and not only in the poetic canon, the set of norms of a given poetic school, but also in the art of a given epoch, viewed as a particular whole' (83).

Shklovsky had maintained that the work of art de-automatised the viewer's perception of art itself, and also his or her experience of reality. Implicit in this is the question: de-automatised from what to what? And thus a space is created for the entry of issues of history and evolution into the theory. In this way, the earlier work of the Formalists led from an analytical and descriptive assessment of the device in the text to a consideration of the evolution of literary features and laws. Jakobson comments:

> In the earlier works of Šklovskij, a poetic work was defined as a mere sum of its artistic devices, while poetic evolution appeared nothing more than a substitution of certain devices. With the further development of Formalism, there arose the accurate conception of a poetic work as a structured system, a regularly ordered hierarchical set of artistic devices. Poetic evolution is a shift in this hierarchy. The hierarchy of artistic devices changes within the framework of a given poetic genre; the change, moreover, affects the hierarchy of poetic genres, and, simultaneously, the distribution of artistic devices among the individual genres. Genres which were originally secondary paths, subsidiary variants, now come to the fore, whereas the canonical genres are pushed toward the rear. (85)

Formalist theory may thus be roughly divided into two areas of enquiry, approximately corresponding to the two phases of development of the theory, though there is much overlap. The first is semiotic, seeing the text as a series of devices or strategies intended to defamiliarise the reader's approach to literature. This is a descriptive and functionalist approach, concerned with features of the text — the literary 'facts' — and how they work in the text.

In this, Formalism rebelled against the traditional and dominant modes of literary criticism of the time, which sought to pin down the meaning of the text in terms of the philosophy apparently articulated in it; the author's biography and psychology as perceived through it; the position of the text in the succession of historical events in its context; and the like. Indeed, Erlich tells us, Jakobson

> described traditional literary history as a 'loose conglomeration of home-bred disciplines', and compared its methods to those of the police 'who, when ordered to arrest a certain person, would take along, to make sure, everybody and everything they happened to find in the culprit's apartment as well as all passers-by encountered in the street'. Likewise, 'the literary historian took indiscriminately in his stride everything that came his way: mores, psychology, politics, philosophy'. (71)

The significance of the *literary* facts for the 'meaning' of the total work became secondary in the early work of the Formalists, though the theorists generally insisted on the integral relationship of form and content (as, indeed, did the Anglo-American New Critics). Formalist analysis of literary texts, therefore, is often a close and detailed examination of such features as specific tropes of language, or metrical patterns.

Later, however, as Eikhenbaum noted in his *Verse Melody*, 'We have to find something related to the *poetic phrase* that does not also lead us away from the poetry itself, something bordering on both phonetics and semantics. This "something" is syntax' ('The Theory of the "Formal Method"' 125). In this way, content (semantics) was to be reintegrated with form (phonetics), without subordinating the latter to the former. 'The emphasis on the inextricable relationship between rhythm and syntax and their interdependence,' says Erlich, 'became the leitmotif of the Formalist study of verse in the mid-twenties' (89).

The desire to identify the nature of the literary text and its 'laws' permits the theory to be described as a poetics of literature. It was this perspective that earned Shklovsky, Tynyanov, and the others the nickname Formalist from their political enemies, who perceived in the attention paid to form and structure a disregard for an ideologically acceptable thematics which would classify literary texts native and foreign as good or bad, according to their conformity with the Stalinist revision of Marxist-Communist theory.

The second area of Formalist inquiry moves toward mimesis, investigating the laws of literary evolution. Noting that certain kinds of literary 'facts' appear, disappear and/or reappear over time, whereas others seem to remain constant, and still others change and apparently undergo a kind of evolution, some of the Formalists set themselves to examine how and why this might be so. In this way, the group's earlier, almost exclusive attention to formal matters and textual features gave way to a theorisation of the literary work as part of literary history, that is, a history of the development of literary forms and features. Eikhenbaum tells us that:

> the original attempt of the Formalists to take a particular structural device and to establish its identity in diverse materials became an attempt to differentiate, to understand, the *function* of a device in each given case. This notion of functional significance was gradually pushed toward the foreground and the original idea of the device pushed into the background. (132)

The move away from describing the devices present in a text (and from Shklovsky's early definition of the literary work as merely the sum of its devices) to analysing their functions in it necessarily invoked a concept of historical evolution, since certain devices may have been used to produce very different effects at different moments in the history of literature. Thus, as Eikhenbaum himself says, 'Work on specific materials compelled us to speak of functions and thus to revise our idea of the device. The theory itself demanded that we turn to history' (132).

So Formalist interest now focused increasingly on the twin issues of literary history — the account of changing forms and structures in literature over time — and of literary evolution — the account of how these forms and structures had changed:

> We were interested in the very process of evolution, in the very *dynamics* of literary form, insofar as it was possible to observe them in the facts of the past. For us, the central problem of the history of literature is the problem of evolution without personality — the study of literature as a *self-formed* social phenomenon. (Eikhenbaum 136)

The intent of the Formalists was thus to make the study of literature more scientific, to replace the biographical, psychological, philosophical, historical and sociological meditations on literary texts with the appropriate object of a literary inquiry: the laws of literature and their history. 'We did not take up questions of the biography and psychology of the artist,' says Eikhenbaum, 'because we assumed that these questions, in themselves serious and complex, must take their places in other science' (136).

An important figure in the study of poetry in this new development of Formalist theory was Yuri Tynyanov, who published *The Problem of Verse Language* in 1924. The book was originally entitled *The Problem of Verse Semantics*, but the publisher took fright at the idea of publishing Tynyanov's work under this title, no doubt because of the increasing scrutiny by Marxist critics and theorists of the field of semantics itself, and their correlation of the latter with the current approved political ideology. In such an intellectual climate, a work that promised to look at semantics as an autonomous field would not be welcome — and the Formalists were already being criticised for their lack of seriousness with regard to Marxist ideology.

Tynyanov's is a rigorous and subtle examination of one of the first and central issues of Formalist theory, namely, the definition of verse language against that of prose. A number of the themes we have already considered with regard to Russian Formalist theory are gathered together in Tynyanov's work, including the relationship of form to content; the isolation of laws pertaining specifically to poetic language; the notion of a dominant which deforms other devices and structures in the text; and the like. Reflecting the new Formalist attention to historical issues, Tynyanov is also concerned to integrate his findings concerning the laws of poetic language into a historical scheme, or 'series', as he called it.[7] Most important, he insists on regarding the poetic text as intrinsically dynamic, and defines it as a *system* whose various parts interact with one another, and function across the entire text:

> The unity of the work is not a closed, symmetrical intactness, but an unfolding, dynamic integrity. Between its elements is not the static sign of equality and addition, but the dynamic sign of correlation and integration.
>
> The form of the literary work must be recognized as a dynamic phenomenon.
>
> This dynamism reveals itself firstly in the constructive principle. Not all factors of a word[8] are equivalent. Dynamic form is not generated by means of combination or merger ... but by means of interaction, and, consequently, the pushing forward of one group of factors at the expense of another. In so doing, the advanced factor deforms the subordinate ones. The sensation of form is always the sensation of flow (and, consequently of the alteration) of correlation between the subordinating, constructive factor and the subordinated factors. (33)

The 'constructive factor', then, is what Eikhenbaum and Jakobson called the dominant, and, like them, Tynyanov links this factor with the notion of history:

> Art lives by means of this interaction and struggle. Without this sensation of subordination and deformation of all factors by the one factor playing the constructive role, there is no fact of art... If

this sensation of the *interaction* of factors disappears (which assumes the compulsory presence of *two* features: the subordinating and the subordinated), the fact of art is obliterated. It becomes automatized.

In this way a historical nuance is introduced into the concept of the 'constructive principle' and the material. (33)

The constructive factor in poetry is rhythm, by which Tynyanov means more than a technical metrics, since, as he points out, rhythm occurs also in prose (54), where, however, its function is different from rhythm in verse. In Tynyanov's view, the literary text is a system in which certain key principles function. In poetry, rhythm is such a principle whose factors Tynyanov summarises as follows:

1. the factor of the unity of the verse series;
2. the factor of its compactness;
3. the factor of vocal material being made dynamic, and
4. the factor of the successiveness of vocal material in verse. (63)

By this, he means, first, that the line (and, ultimately, the whole poetic text) is to be viewed as integral and unified; second, that it is compact; third, that the patterns of sound and metre are organised in such a way as to produce and fulfil certain expectations in the poem; and, finally, that those patterns themselves are alternated and varied throughout. Sosa and Harvey, in the introduction to their translation of Tynyanov's book, summarise Tynyanov's findings thus: 'rhythm is the constructive factor of verse, dominating and turning all laws of prosaic semantics in a particular direction, that direction which is functionally advanced in the particular poem' (17).

The poem is seen, then, as a textual system consisting of a dominant (generically, in poetry, this feature is the factor of rhythm) which organises and deforms all others in relation to itself. This may sound a rather odd way in which to read any sort of literary work — to see it as a bundle of strategies interacting with one another, and apparently independent of any clear semantic meaning. The Formalists addressed this difficulty by way of the notion of motivation, which was particularly developed in their theorisation of narrative. Shklovsky defined it as the 'extraliterary...explanation of plot construction' (Steiner 51–2), that is, the story (*fabula*) told in chronological causative sequence. This story, however, is merely the pretext (the motivation) for a plot (*syuzhet*) which takes the events of the story and reworks them, so that the extraliterary narrative *account* actually becomes the literary exploration of narrative *technique*.

In this way, theme or content remains a part of the literary work, but it is backgrounded as the *raison d'être* for the form. Nonetheless, the acceptance of such motivation as present in the total meaning of the literary text means that motivation itself becomes part of literary history: certain themes or stories are thus made available for study as they appear and reappear historically, and as they undergo changes or modifications. One might think, for instance, of the changes rung on the Cinderella story, from the earliest versions of this fairy tale to its manifestations in romances and soap operas today. These sorts of motivational stories form the basis for studies such as *The Morphology of the Folktale*, in which Vladimir Propp investigates the limited number of possible structural formulae present in folktale, and how these undergo multifarious changes and inflections in their actual recounting.

The notion of a motivational theme, moreover, allows a theorist like Tynyanov to discuss the 'oscillation' in the meaning of words at the semantic level of the poetic text. Indeed, he devotes the second chapter of his study of verse language to the questions of what he calls 'lexical colouring' and the effect on meaning   of verse and its dominants.

With the acknowledgment of the presence of a theme or reference to some order of knowledge and reality outside the text, Russian Formalist theory also admitted a degree of mimetic value. This increased as the Formalists turned more and more to questions to do with the evolution of literary form and other issues of historical import. Nonetheless, Formalist theory remained emphatically interested in the structures and dynamics of literary language and form.

Formalism in Practice

The Brown Snake

I walked to the green gum-tree
Because the day was hot;
A snake could be anywhere
But that time I forgot.

The Duckmaloi lazed through the valley
In amber pools like tea
From some old fossicker's billy,
And I walked under the tree.

Blue summer smoked on Bindo,
It lapped me warm in its waves,
And when that snake hissed up
Under the shower of leaves

Huge, high as my waist,
Rearing with lightning's tongue,
So brown with heat like the fallen
Dry sticks it hid among,

I thought the earth itself
Under the green gum-tree,
All in the sweet of summer
Reached out to strike at me.

                              Douglas Stewart

Douglas Stewart's poem, set in Australia (the Duckmaloi River and Mt Bindo are to be found in the Blue Mountains of New South Wales),[9] appears to tell a simple narrative: the speaker (presumably male), seeking shelter from the heat of the day, enters the shadow of a green gum-tree, but forgets that 'A snake could be anywhere'. He is therefore taken so completely by surprise when a brown snake rears up before him that it seems to him as if nature itself has set an ambush for him. It might be said of this narrative that it has two motivations. The first is a local or geographical one, namely, that summer is typically a dangerous season in most parts of Australia, since it is the time when the various venomous and poisonous reptiles to be found on the continent are most active. From this perspective, then, the lines 'A snake could be anywhere/ But that time I forgot' signal a possible interpretation of the poem as a moral lesson: forgetting about snakes in the hot season in Australia can be fatal.

The motivation derives from a constellation of associations centred on the snake in Western cultural assumptions and myths. These see the snake, on the one hand, as intrinsically wily and evil,[10] as the tool of Satan, and as the cause of humanity's expulsion in shame from the Garden of Eden into a world of difficulty, pain and death. On the other hand, however, the serpent is also associated with wisdom and with benefit to humanity: even in Genesis, it persuades Eve to disobey God's command in order to gain knowledge of sorts. In the classical tradition the serpent was associated with oracular prophecy and with medicinal healing. In both cases, though, the snake, whether hostile or friendly, is conceived as alien to humanity.

Seen from this point of view, Stewart's poem ironises the speaker's 'forgetting' of wisdom and his regaining of it suddenly when the snake rises before him. Moreover, the snake is associated with nature — 'the earth itself' — whereas the human speaker, careless and jaunty at the outset, is defined as an intruder. The poem thus enters a long cultural and literary tradition — and this is its second motivation — in which humanity's true 'home' is conceived to be elsewhere, and the earth is seen to be a place of exile or imprisonment. That this was also a definition of Australia itself during the nineteenth century, when it was essentially a prison island to which English convicts and ne'er-do-wells were sent, has its own resonance in the structure of meaning of this poem: the speaker, though evidently an inhabitant of Australia, is not 'of' Australia in the same sense that the landscape and the snake, the only other moving, living creature in the poem, are.

In terms of a Formalist reading, however, these two ways of understanding the central image of the rearing, striking snake are not helpful in understanding how this poem functions as a literary text, that is, as a system of devices interacting with one another. To read the poem in this way, we might notice that the text commences with 'I' and closes with 'me', a pattern repeated in the final stanza. Grammatically, then, the poem begins with the first person as subject, as *doing* (walking, perceiving, feeling), but it ends with the first person as object, as *that to which deeds are done*. The first appearance of the objective form of the first person occurs in the third stanza: 'It lapped *me* warm in its waves'. Here, the 'me' has a semantic colouring that is different from that of 'I thought the earth itself/ ... Reached out to strike at *me*.' In the first case, the objective first person form is perceived as part of a maternal, enfolding nature, whereas in the second, it is seen as alienated from, and victimised by, that same nature. It is partly in this shift of semantic colouring that the sense of betrayal in the poem is located.

The third stanza also performs the function of dividing two categories of image in the poem. In the earlier part, the images of nature are humanised, in consonance with the speaker's forgetting that 'A snake could be anywhere.' Thus, the Duckmaloi River, whose very name suggests the imposition upon nature of categories and nomenclatures that are actually foreign to nature, is transformed from a body of water into 'amber pools like tea/ From some old fossicker's billy,' an ironic metaphor, since tea is not native to Australia, while the term 'fossicker', signifying a prospector for precious minerals, suggests someone who disturbs rather than complements the natural context. In other words, the speaker *reconstructs* nature so that it takes a human, familiar face.

However, with the appearance of the snake, nature returns to its component features — leaves, the 'lightning's tongue' of the snake, the serpent's brownness, heat, dry sticks. It is humans who try to combine and manipulate the elements of nature into some meaningful relationship — meaningful, that is, in terms of human desires and ambitions; nature itself simply functions. The images of the second part of the poem are, consequently, less integrated, isolating the 'me' of the closing line still further. In this vision of nature as made up of component parts only loosely adjoining, just as the leaves and the dry sticks are simply a convenient camouflage for the snake, the human subject has no place, and cannot integrate the various elements in order to give them a coherent meaning. The response is terror, and a sense of vulnerability.

The central stanza of the poem serves yet another function. It facilitates the sudden shift of effect in the metrical scheme. A metrical analysis of the poem shows that its basic line is an iambic (˘ ´) trimeter (three feet to the line). A lilting, but nonetheless somewhat disturbing, because irregular, effect is created by the insertion of other metres, for example, an anapaestic foot (˘˘|´), or by the reversal of the iamb to create a trochee (´ ˘), as in 'Thĕ Dúckmălŏi lázed'thróugh thĕ'vállĕy.' (We might note here, too, that the trimeter becomes a tetrameter by the addition of a further metrical foot.) By and large, though, the metre of the earlier stanzas tends to place accented syllables *after* unaccented ones in each foot. The second half of the third stanza, however, breaks abruptly into this pattern, disordering it so that the kind of metre foregrounded in the remainder of the poem is more heavily accented, until the closing stanza, where the iambic metre begins to reassert itself.

Thus, the earlier part of the poem consists of a rather sing-song metre whose predictability suggests the security of the speaker in this section of the text, but whose occasional variations set up disturbances in the reading of the poem. The second half of the third stanza suddenly violates this metre, 'de-automatising' it as it were, first by a series of accented monosyllables ('Ánd whén thát snáke híssed úp'),[11] followed by feet whose gradual return to the staple iambic metre becomes an ironic comment on the fresh perception by the speaker of his place in the landscape.

The earlier interruptions and violations of the poem's basic iambic trimeter may be understood in two further ways. In the first, we can imagine a certain external psychological reality motivating the text's narrative account. That is, though we may initially read the poem as a simple story about the speaker's carelessness and his consequent fright upon encountering the snake, in fact the story is told to us *after* his experience. We may then read the metrical violations as reflecting the speaker's still reverberating reaction to the encounter. The changes in metre then signify a psychological and emotional state projected retrospectively upon that part of the narrative preceding the actual encounter in the poem. This psycho-emotional reaction then coincides with the events of the story from the end of the third stanza, which explains the somewhat more disordered and heavily accented metrical scheme in the latter part of the text.

The second way of understanding the metrical irregularities of this poem, however, is to conceive of them as a particular strategy designed to unsettle the reader. The key to this strategy is the critical disturbance of the metre in the second half of the third stanza. The de-automatisation of the fundamental iambic trimeter takes its origin here, so that metrical variations and violations radiate from this centre toward both the opening and the closing of the text. In this way, the psycho-emotional motivation of the first explanation coincides with and appears to justify the manipulation of the poem's metre.

The first two stanzas of the poem are constructed so that each is made up of a single sentence. By contrast, the other three stanzas are syntactically and grammatically interlinked, together forming a long sentence that runs through to the end of the poem. The effect of this manipulation of the grammatical and stanzaic segments of the poem is twofold. In the first place, it disengages the last three stanzas — in which is described the encounter with the snake and the terrible realisation or perception it brings — from the first two, emphasising their functions as setting the background or scene for the rest of the poem.

In the second place, this division causes us to perceive the lack of logic in the first two stanzas. There is no strong relationship between the first two lines of the first stanza and the second two:

> I walked to the green gum-tree
> Because the day was hot;
> A snake could be anywhere
> But that time I forgot.

The reader makes the connection between the speaker's seeking shelter under the gum-tree, and the subsequent two statements of the text — that 'A snake could be anywhere' and 'But that time I forgot' — to create a sense of anticipation based on the relationship of these otherwise logically unrelated elements.

The logic is more patently problematic in the second stanza:

> The Duckmaloi lazed through the valley
> In amber pools like tea
> From some old fossicker's billy,
> And I walked under the tree.

Here, the 'And' of the fourth line connects a description of the Duckmaloi River irrelevantly with the detailing of the fact that the speaker walks 'under the tree'. Of course, the reader is free to suppose, from this connective, that the tree may be located alongside or near the river, but there is no positive indication in the text itself that this is so.

The irrelevance of the connection is repeated forcefully in the third stanza, when the focus moves suddenly from the description of the summer on Mt Bindo to the appearance of the snake. However, whereas in the earlier part of the text the casual nature of the logical connections symbolically parallels the casual attitude of the speaker, who takes for granted his right to be present in this landscape, in this part of the poem the disjunction of logic assists the effect of shock when the snake suddenly appears. For, although it has already been foreshadowed by lines three and four of the poem, the reliance of the poem so far on slight logical connections tends to diffuse the sense of warning established in the first stanza. The sequence of diffusion followed by shocked realisation is further assisted by the emphasised lilt of the poem's metrical scheme, and its sudden abandonment, also in this third stanza.

The poem thus establishes at the outset a number of metrical, logical, syntactical and grammatical features which it abruptly changes or abandons in the second part of the third stanza. In terms of Russian Formalist theory, we may say that these earlier features are set up in order to become automatised by the text. These features are tied to a conceptual or semantic level which suggests complacency about the human factor in nature. The poem's dominant, then, is a reversal or contradiction of those features, one which, on the semantic level, disrupts and questions that complacency.

Identifying the dynamic of this poem also helps us to place it in terms of literary tradition. The idea of nature as healer and restorative derives from the philosophy and writings of nineteenth-century Romanticism, and was an idea that was already challenged in the nineteenth century by figures such as Alfred Lord Tennyson. He saw a different possibility: 'Nature, red in tooth and claw/ With ravine' (*In Memoriam* 56.15–16). Stewart juxtaposes both myths of nature, so that in the first two stanzas of his poem the speaker is lulled and comforted by Romantic nature, nature the healer and protector of all creatures, while in the last three stanzas the speaker is shocked into an awareness of a different kind of nature, nature hostile, defensive and predatory.

Also grounded in Romantic ideology is the shift from subject to object. Romantic poetry and theory treat the poet-speaker as perceiving subject, conceptually aware of, and emotionally sensitive to, the delicate structures and dynamics of nature. Where the poet-speaker is defined as object (as, for instance, at the end of Wordsworth's 'She Dwelt Among the Untrodden Ways'), it is in order to re-orient his or her perception as subject, to see things differently.

Stewart's poem locates itself in that tradition, for the sudden rearing of the snake indeed alters the speaker's perception of nature, and of his own place, as a human being, in nature. However, the poem also emphasises more strongly the speaker's sense of himself as object of nature's attack, and thus identifies the text as post-Romantic, and as in some sense parodic of Romantic ideology.

Stewart's poem also encapsulates two hundred years of response to Australia itself. For many of the new inhabitants, the island continent seemed a new Eden, free of the constraints that marked European life, despite Australia's beginnings as a convict colony. For others, however, and especially for the convicts themselves, Australia must have seemed hostile and threatening. The art of early immigrants into Australia reflects this duality of outlook: many landscapes of professedly Australian scenes in fact reflect traditions of English and European landscape painting, and in some instances depict trees that were not native to Australia, and had not yet been imported. This example is a good illustration of the Formalist idea that art and life become automatised, and that a de-automatisation is necessary so that we can once again see things clearly, without the encrustations of familiarity. Given something new to look at and understand, some of the early Australian artists preferred automatisation; others — the majority — of course embraced the opportunity to break free of European and English traditions and codes.

Stewart's poem also points to such a de-automatisation: in his text, nature, taken for granted, is allowed to reassert itself in the speaker's eyes, and to show that, for all the history of domestication of the land, nature remains alien, separate and potentially dangerous.

Notwithstanding Eikhenbaum's claim that Formalism moved inevitably toward a historical mode because of its own internal logic, it is possible to argue that the *Opoyaz* group was subjected to great pressure ideologically and politically to conform to the historicising tendencies of Marxist theory, whether political or literary. The régime saw in Formalism potential subversion, particularly in its refusal to accept the crude Marxist theoretical view of literature espoused by its ideologues: these used a simple mimetic model which saw the literary text as a mirror of historical, social and economic events.[12]

In 1928, towards the end of the second phase of the development of Formalist theory, Jakobson and Tynyanov proposed a new departure for Formalism:

In a set of mathematically terse propositions the signatories repudiated doctrinaire Formalism, which abstracted the esthetic 'series' from other domains of culture, as well as mechanical causalism, which denied the inner dynamism and the specificity of each individual realm. 'Literary history', they declared, 'is closely bound up with other historic "series". Each of the series is

characterized by peculiar structural laws. Without an inquiry into these laws, it is impossible to establish the connection between the literary "series" and other sets of cultural phenomena. To study the system of systems, while ignoring the internal laws of each individual system, is a grave methodological error.'
(Erlich, *Russian Formalism* 134)

Unfortunately, the possibilities of this new direction for Formalism were not explored, for the theory was criticised and condemned by the Stalinist régime, while the proponents of the theory were effectively silenced. The notion that a culture may be regarded as a 'system of systems', however, remained an important feature of the newly emerging field of structuralist theory being developed by Jakobson in Prague.

Nevertheless, Formalism itself was not totally extinguished in the Soviet Union. Several of the theoreticians continued to write, albeit more guardedly and with a weather eye towards the ideological and political realities of the period. And the theory has re-emerged in other forms since World War II: as Soviet structuralism, at the University of Moscow, for example, and as a semiotics of literature, film and culture at the University of Tartu in Estonia. Scholars in this revived and revised Russian Formalism include Boris Uspensky and Yuri Lotman.

The Formalists thus remained committed to the principle of the semiotic study of the dynamics of the literary text, and, particularly during the second phase of the group's history, integrated this 'formal' emphasis into a theory of evolution and of historical-cultural dynamism. The latter was partly an attempt to develop a semiotics of culture, and partly a mimetic reading of the literary text in terms of the cultural (historical, political, social) context. It may be argued, however, that this later development was forced upon the Formalists by political events in the Soviet Union, and by the historical emphasis of Marxist philosophy. It is ironic, therefore, as a number of commentators on Russian Formalism has pointed out, that a theoretical school which began by denying the importance of history and of external reality to literary study should have ended in a dissolution brought about by actual events of history and external political reality.

Notes

1.   The transliteration of Russian names poses something of a problem, since there does not appear to be a standard orthography for the transliteration of Slavic names and words. I have elected to follow the practice of many accounts in English of Formalism by Anglicising the spelling of names

and terms. Authorities on Russian literature and poetics cited below, for instance, Erlich, Steiner, and Matejka and Pomorska can be inconsistent in their use of a Slavicised orthography to represent the Russian originals. Erlich, for instance, throughout his book on Russian Formalism represents the guttural with an 'x', as, for instance, in the name 'Ejxenbaum'. Yet, in his introduction to the third edition he represents the same sound with 'kh' in the name 'Mikhail Bakhtin' (10), which is, however, spelled 'Mixail Baxtin' in the Matejka-Pomorska collection. Steiner, by contrast, represents the guttural by 'ch' in the name 'Ejchenbaum.' To aid the reader in correlating the different spellings of names and words important in Formalism, the following brief list might be of use.

š   pronounced 'sh', as in 'Šklovskij' (Shklovsky)
č   pronounced 'ch', as in 'Čajkovskij' (Tchaikovsky)
ž   pronounced 'zh', as in 'Žirmunskij' (Zhirmunsky)
c   pronounced 'ts', as in 'Trockij' (Trotsky)
j   a palatal glide, pronounced as consonantal 'y', as in 'Jakubinskij'
ë   an indeterminate sound, somewhere between 'ah' and 'uh', as in 'Bogatyrëv' (Bogatyrov or Bogatyrev)

2. This acronym stands for The Society for the Study of Poetic Language.
3. Bakhtin's work is considered below, in Chapter 6, 'Poetry and History'.
4. According to Erlich, after Jakobson's departure 'there was a noticeable slackening of the Circle's activities. A sharp split within the Circle between two philosophical orientations, the "Marxist" and the "Husserlian" led to further weakening and to eventual disintegration of the first Formalist nucleus' (85, footnote).
5. This statement is to be found in 'Sterne's *Tristram Shandy*: Stylistic Commentary', included in the edition by Lemon and Reis of Formalist essays cited in the Suggestions for Further Reading, 57.
6. In this emphasis by Shklovsky on technique and device in the work of art, Formalist theory foreshadows Derrida's deconstructive interest in the tropes of language.
7. Sosa and Harvey, in their translation of Tynyanov's work, note that the Russian term *rjad* can mean 'series', on the one hand, and 'order' or 'realm', on the other.
8. Probably a printer's error for 'work'.
9. I am indebted for this information to my colleague Mr W.S. Cooper.
10. The seventeenth-century King James translation of the Bible says the serpent was 'more subtle than any beast of the field' (Genesis 3:1): 'subtle' carried negative connotations in the language of the day.
11. The rising inflection of this line, if read aloud, imitates the rearing of the snake; but it also imposes additional stress on each monosyllable, so that the earlier iambic becomes a background against which the spondaic (˝) feet make their effect.
12. Erlich observes that Trotsky, recognised, however grudgingly, the achievements and value of the work of the Formalists, but regarded the theory as defective in its response to and application of historical materialism.

Suggestions for Further Reading

Primary

Bakhtin, M.M., and P.N. Medvedev. *The Formal Method in Literary Scholarship: A Critical Introduction to Sociological Poetics.* Trans. Albert J. Wehrle. Cambridge, Mass. and London: Harvard University Press, 1985.

Bann, Stephen, and John E. Bowlt, eds. *Russian Formalism: A Collection of Articles and Texts in Translation.* Edinburgh: Scottish Academic Press, 1973.

Eichenbaum, Boris. 'The Theory of the "Formal Method"'. Lee T. Lemon and Marion J. Reis, eds. *Russian Formalist Criticism: Four Essays.* Lincoln: University of Nebraska Press, 1965. 99–139.

Matejka, Ladislav, and Irwin R. Titunik, eds. *Semiotics of Art: Prague School Contributions.* Cambridge, Mass., and London: MIT, 1976.

— and Krystyna Pomorska, eds. *Readings in Russian Poetics: Formalist and Structuralist Views.* Michigan Slavic Contributions 8. Cambridge, Mass.: MIT; Ann Arbor: Michigan Slavic Publications, 1978.

O'Toole, L.M., and Ann Shukman, eds. *Russian Poetics in Translation, Vol. 4: Formalist Theory.* Oxford: Holdan Books, 1977.

— *Russian Poetics in Translation, Vol. 5: Formalism: History, Comparison, Genre.* Oxford: Holdan Books, 1978.

Shklovsky, Victor. 'Art as Technique'. Lee T. Lemon and Marion J. Reis, eds. *Russian Formalist Criticism: Four Essays.* Lincoln: University of Nebraska Press, 1965. 3–24.

Smith, G.S., ed. and trans. *Russian Poetics in Translation, Vol. 7: Metre, Rhythm, Stanza, Rhyme.* Oxford: Holdan Books, 1980.

Tomashevsky, Boris. 'Thematics'. Lee T. Lemon and Marion J. Reis, eds. *Russian Formalist Criticism: Four Essays.* Lincoln: University of Nebraska Press, 1965. 61–95.

Tynianov, Yuri. *The Problem of Verse Language.* Ed. and trans. Michael Sosa and Brent Harvey. Ann Arbor: Ardis, 1981.

Secondary

Abrams, M.H. 'Russian Formalism'. *A Glossary of Literary Terms.* 4th edn. New York: Holt, Rinehart & Winston, 1981.

Bennett, Tony. *Formalism and Marxism.* London and New York: Methuen, 1979.

Erlich, Victor. 'Russian Formalism'. *Princeton Encyclopedia of Poetry and Poetics.* Ed. Alex Preminger, Frank J. Warnke and O.B. Hardison, Jr. Princeton University Press, 1974. London and Basingstoke: Macmillan, 1975.

— *Russian Formalism: History-Doctrine.* New Haven and London: Yale University Press, 1965, 1981.

Jackson, Robert Louis, and Stephen Rudy, eds. *Russian Formalism: A Retrospective Glance. A Festschrift in Honor of Victor Erlich.* New Haven: Yale Center for International and Area Studies, 1985.

Jameson, Fredric. *The Prison-House of Language: A Critical Account of Structuralism and Russian Formalism.* Princeton: Princeton University Press, 1972.

Jefferson, Ann. 'Russian Formalism'. Jefferson and Robey. 16–37.

Selden, Raman. 'Russian Formalism'. 6–22.
Steiner, Peter. *Russian Formalism: A Metapoetics*. Ithaca and London: Cornell University Press, 1984.
Thompson, Ewa M. *Russian Formalism and Anglo-American New Criticism: A Comparative Study*. The Hague and Paris: Mouton, 1971.

6

Poetry and History

The poem is not only a literary fact, but also a social one. That is, the poem is produced within a context which includes the life of the author, the audience for whom he or she writes, and the background relationships of various social, historical and political factors. The poem, therefore, is enmeshed in circumstance, both in its production by the poet and its reception by the reader. Such circumstances include sets of relations among author, audience, social context, the political and ideological complexion of these, and their position in the sequence of events which is called history. The presence of these in the poem, even if understood only as implicit, raises certain issues which various literary theories tackle in different ways.

Our division of literary theory into the broad categories of mimetic and semiotic theories highlights the sometimes problematic relation of history to the text. Approaches which emphasise the semiotic element, like New Criticism, incline to move history to the margins in order to focus attention on questions about what the text means in terms of its sign systems and dynamics. By contrast, those which stress the mimetic, like gender theory (see Chapter 7), incorporate, in differing ways, a number of historical factors: such theories assume that, as part of its meaning, the text refers, to a greater or lesser degree, to events, ideas, personalities, structures, relationships or other sorts of facts outside itself.

In some instances — Russian Formalism is a case in point — a purely semiotic approach has yielded to a mimetic one in which historical events or dynamics have become central issues. In other instances, the way in which history is dealt with may pose other difficulties. We have noted, for instance, that, because it foregrounds history as synchronic rather than diachronic, classical structuralism is hard put to explain evolutionary changes except as a series of synchronic moments.

History functions as a factor in all literary theory, whether by its explicit incorporation into a theoretical framework, or by its attempted exclusion. And, though much may be made of texts as transcending history, as speaking to all readers of all times, the literary work takes its existence, first, within the history of the author's life, and, second, within the culture and its history.[1]

Some current theory, however, problematises the notion of history itself. The term commonly refers to events of the past recounted sequentially and in chronological order, presumably in an objective manner. However, as historiography, the study of the writing of histories, early discovered, objectivity can be said to be virtually absent in the writing of history. Though a certain body of facts may exist, the way in which these are selected and ordered in various historical accounts can produce singularly different versions of 'history'. For example, consider the way in which a standard Anglo-American history of World War II might recount the events of the war, compared with such a history written by someone sympathetic to the Nazi cause and ideology. The overthrow of the Third Reich would be seen, in the first account, as a triumph, the liberation of the world from forces of tyranny, cruelty and perversion both intellectual and physical. In the second account, the Allied Forces themselves would be perceived as tyrannical, intolerant and incapable of seeing the justice and rectitude of the Nazi enterprise. Similarly, a French account of the war would see it rather differently from an English or an American one, since France was one of the battlegrounds on which the fighting actually took place.

Even the notion of the historical fact can itself be open to question, since many such 'facts' are actually conjectures made by historians from other 'facts'. Moreover, as new evidence comes to light through archaeological or archival research, ideas which have possessed the status of facts become subject to change, and are suddenly no longer seen in this way.

Theorist-historians such as Hayden White, raise another problem relevant to the question of the objectivity, the 'factuality', of history. As the historian moves from the area of annals (the listing of events) into the area of history (the marshalling of these into a sequence which tells a story and explains those events in relation to one another), he or she also moves into the field of literary narrative. The facts of history, such as they are, then become subject to the codes and exigencies of narrative, and may be read, in fact, as *literature* rather than history. This is obviously important in relation to prose fiction, since, taken to its logical extreme, it blurs the distinction between historical and literary (that is, fictional) narrative. It also has significance for the reading of poetry.

In this chapter, we will review briefly several literary theories which address the relationship of the poetic text to history more directly than some of the theories with which we have so far dealt. These historicist approaches may be conceived as falling into two groups: the 'old' historicism, and the 'new' Marxist and post-Marxist historicism.[2] The term 'old historicism', however, should not be understood to mean that the approaches grouped under this heading are now obsolete. Many are still practised, and are capable of yielding interesting and subtle readings of literary texts.

The historicist approach to the literary text may be traced back to the nineteenth century and its interest in writing (that is, constructing) history.[3] Of course, an interest in history was neither new in nor unique to this century. One of the oldest key texts in Western culture, the Bible, for instance, exhibits an interest in documenting historical events and explaining them, in terms of God's will and humanity's obedience to that will. And the history of European thought and writing thereafter yields many accounts of history and attempts to theorise it. Machiavelli's *The Prince* (1573), for example, is an attempt to understand the cycles of history and to show how the ambitious ruler might learn from these and use them to his or her advantage. Gibbon's massive account of Roman history, *The Decline and Fall of the Roman Empire*, published between 1776 and 1788, marked another milestone in the European interest in history, and in the understanding of history as a series of lessons for the present and the future.

The appearance in 1859 of Darwin's *Origin of Species* prompted a new wave of interest in history. Darwin's work was really concerned with matters pertaining to biology. However, in its attention to the question of the survival of biological species, it had implications for the notion of history in general. Human cultural history could be understood as paralleling the processes by which nature selected certain species for survival according to their adaptability to changing conditions and their consequent ability to evolve into different forms. Writers began to address themselves to the task of analysing the factors of history, rather than seeing it as a series of events from which certain moral and/or political principles might be deduced. Indeed, the nineteenth century saw the rise of the historian as a professional and academic figure. From this canonisation of history developed also other new fields related to history, for instance, archaeology, palaeontology, philology and anthropology. History was raised to the level of a science.

The historicist approach to literature and to the literary text took two main forms. The first, which we might call the genetic approach, saw the literary text as descending from certain antecedent texts. It was chiefly concerned with tracing thematic or generic links among texts, creating 'families' through their relationships of ancestry and descent, and showing the development of unfolding theme or genre.

Another aspect of the genetic approach is the study of literary influences. This study makes more explicit the family relationship among texts, for it seeks the specific sources for ideas, images, or even turns of phrase in one text which may be derived from one or more others.

The genetic approach makes two major assumptions. The first is that of contact, whether direct or indirect. It presupposes, and then proves, that the author of one work came into contact with that of another (or several others), either through antecedence, reading the work of earlier writers; or through linearity, knowing other writers personally and deriving ideas or methods from them through this familiarity; or reading the work of contemporary writers and in this way absorbing their ideas or methods. In this way, the principle of intertextuality is given a specifically historical bias.

The other major assumption is that of periodisation. The genetic approach creates historical categories among which is to be distributed the entire canon of literary works. This assumption is still at work in universities which teach courses in mediaeval or Renaissance literature, for instance, as well as in histories of literature. Such courses and books assume that texts produced within a particular synchronic moment (the Middle Ages, the Renaissance) all have something in common, on the one hand, while, on the other, they possess discernible and important differences from texts produced in a different synchronic moment, no matter how close to one another in time each of these historical moments might be.

This raises a number of problems of classification, for while some writers may be inserted comfortably within such periodic categories, others, particularly those whose work is not typical of the period, or who may have written at marginal or transitional historical moments, are much harder to categorise. Was Dante a mediaeval or a Renaissance writer? He exhibits characteristics of both, since he shares much of the mediaeval ideology of earlier writers, but, at the same time, there are elements in his work which question that ideology in a manner that foreshadows the Renaissance. Was Thomas Gray a poet of the eighteenth-century Enlightenment or did he belong to the Romantic school? Gray belongs, in his technique of versification, to the eighteenth century, but some of his attitudes and ideas tend to align him with the Romantics.

The patterns created by the periodisation of history are intended both to provide an account of the historical sequencing of successions of writers, and to explain their relationship to one another in terms of evolutionary development. In order to deal with such questions as we have asked above in relation to Dante and Gray, the genetic approach often creates intermediate categories ('late mediaeval' or 'early modern'), a strategy which both complicates and blurs the patterns of periodisation. A further strategy that is frequently marshalled to cope with the classification of otherwise intractable authors and works is the tracing of influences, which we have already noted. The difficulties of clearly and simply categorising a poet like Gray, for example, can be explained away by showing that his education and social class inclined him towards the Neoclassicist ideology of the Enlightenment, but that events occurring in society, together with the emergent school of Romantic poets, affected him so that his poetry exhibits Romantic as well as Neoclassical traits.

Associated with the genetic approach is that of textual or bibliographical analysis. This is painstaking scholarship which traces the history of the individual text, establishing, where appropriate, the 'correct' version.[4] This form of analysis is also used to identify authorship in works of questionable attribution, or in anonymous works. An industry has grown up in Shakespeare scholarship, for instance, specialising in the identification of 'authentic' Shakespearean elements not only in the canon of works attributed to him, but also in other, collaborated material. Thus, scholars can show that the plays *The Two Noble Kinsmen* and *Henry VIII*, hitherto supposed part of Shakespeare's works, are in fact not entirely by Shakespeare, while the anonymous *Play of Sir Thomas More* can be shown to include material written by Shakespeare, among others. This kind of scholarship employs historical data, such as information about the occasions of composition and circumstances of performance of these plays, as well as a stylistic semiotic analysis which assists the textual scholar in identifying the word usage and grammatical constructions characteristic of a certain writer.

The second major historicist approach contextualised the literary text, and did so in two ways. In the first instance, it argued that the literary work was part of the writer's life, and therefore bore a particular relationship to it. This attitude towards the literary text reinforced the Romantic view of the author or poet as a special individual whose perceptions of life are more profound and complex, as well as more sensitive and emotional, than those of most people. Such a writer, it was supposed, would inevitably set down in his or her work what he or she saw and experienced. As a consequence, the literary work came to be read as a biographical document.

This approach was sharpened and emphasised by the advent of Freudian psychoanalytic theory, whose focus is the psycho-emotional history of the individual, expressed through certain behavioural patterns and through his or her dreams and fantasies. Psychoanalytic theory accordingly takes the literary text to be a sort of dream accessible to its particular form of analysis. The text can thus be construed as a clue to the writer's personality and psychic structures — and problems.

Such an application of history, specifically biographical history, to the literary text carries with it a certain number of difficulties. First, it can — especially in the hands of a reader prone to simplify and thus possibly to vulgarise this approach — ignore the fact that the literary text is *constructed* in quite a deliberate and conscious manner, and is not simply a transparent vehicle through which the writer's personality, experiences and psyche can be seen and understood in the same way as, say, certain parapraxes (the so-called 'Freudian slips') might be. The best psychoanalytic readings of literary texts, by contrast, take the constructedness of the text into account, and read it as a strategy of defence or projection intended, on the one hand, to disguise and protect the writer's psyche, and, on the other, to provide fulfilment of certain wishes or needs of the writer.

A second difficulty of the biographical approach is made clear by the case in which not all the facts of the writer's life may be known. Shakespeare again provides us with an instructive example. Although there is some documentary evidence regarding the life of William Shakespeare — parish records, bills of sale, his will, information provided in the writing of his contemporaries, and so on — by and large the details of his existence are simply unknown to us. This means that Shakespeare's biography cannot be used to confirm certain 'facts' — that is, issues or ideas — in his literary work. The danger of the biographical approach, however, is that it can easily be reversed: instead of finding in the text a reflection of the details of the author's life, the incautious reader can attempt to construct that life from the details of the text. Consequently, much has been written about Shakespeare the man that takes as its point of origin material in his plays and poetry. Debate still rages, for instance, about Shakespeare's sexuality, since his sonnets are written for the most part to a young man, but also to a dark-complexioned woman. However, Shakespeare's heterosexuality, homosexuality or bisexuality can remain only an object of conjecture, since, aside from the known facts of Shakespeare's marriage and his fathering of children, there is no final, incontrovertible evidence outside the literary texts to be found for one or other sexual orientation. The literary text, then, may bear only a rather tenuous or devious relationship to any kind of reality outside itself.

The text may also be contextualised as a social and historical document. That is, the work can be seen as mirroring events in the society and time of the writer. Sometimes this approach is overtly historicist: it looks for clues regarding the period in the text. Thus, for instance, an Elizabethan sonnet may be dated by explicit or implicit (sometimes only inferential) references to natural, historical, political or social events, such as an eclipse, a war, a change of monarch or a royal wedding, known to have happened around the time of composition. At other times, the contextualisation works through gradations of complexity, such as changes in the language (for instance, new words entering it), evolutions of forms (generic or grammatical), and the like.

This sort of approach is exemplified by the commentary on Sonnet 30 of Sir Philip Sidney's *Astrophil and Stella* in William A. Ringler Jr's edition of Sidney's poetry:

> Whether the Turkish new-moone minded be
>   To fill his hornes this yeare on Christian coast;
>   How *Poles'* right king meanes, without leave of hoast,
> To warme with ill-made fire cold *Moscovy*;
> If French can yet three parts in one agree;
>   What now the Dutch in their full diets boast;
>   How *Holland* hearts, now so good townes be lost,
> Trust in the shade of pleasing *Orange* tree;
>   How *Ulster* likes of that same golden bit,
> Wherewith my father once made it halfe tame;
> If in the Scottishe Court be weltring yet;
> These questions busie wits to me do frame;
>   I, cumbred with good maners, answer do,
>   But know not how, for still I thinke of you.

Ringler's note on this poem begins: 'The seven questions asked by "busie wits", the politically-minded gentlemen of Astrophil's acquaintance, refer to the posture of international affairs at a particular time — "this yeare" and "now" (lines 2 and 6); since all seven questions would have been topical only during the summer of 1582, Sidney must have written the sonnet at that time'.[5] Ringler goes on to identify the events to which the poem refers. In this treatment of Sidney's poems, we can see in operation several techniques of the historicist approach. They are: the identification of information in the lines of poetry with actual events occurring in the real world at the time; the use of this correlation to date a specific sonnet; and, in Ringler's commentary on *Astrophil and Stella*, an identification of Astrophil, the speaker of the poems, with Sidney himself, and of Stella, the beloved to whom the poems are addressed, with Lady Penelope Rich, a woman whom Sidney turned down as a marriage prospect but with whom he later fell in love — at least, according to the events described in the sonnet sequence.

This 'old' historicism, therefore, makes strongly mimetic assumptions about the poetic text. It requires the text to take its place within particular historical categories, and demands, moreover, that it fulfil a sort of photographic function, by means of which both/either historical and/or biographical facts become imprinted upon the text, so that it serves as a more or less accurate index of events in society and/or in the poet's life at the time. Though it is still widely practised and still produces fine scholarship and analysis of literary texts, this historicist approach competes in many quarters with Marxist and post-Marxist historicist strategies.

The chief difficulty with the 'old' historicism is the relatively unquestioning connection it makes between the literary text and its context, whether biographical or social. It does not, for instance, consider how the distribution of literacy among the population might well affect the *kind* of poem that is written. Seen from this perspective, what might appear, in an 'old' historicist reading, to be simply a dominant fashion during a particular epoch — the sonnet, say, during the reign of Elizabeth I in England — may in fact be a literary form or genre rooted in the domination of the literary scene by a particular class. Such a form, therefore, would tend to articulate and privilege the ideologies and concerns of that class.

This latter sort of approach was pioneered by another important writer and thinker of the nineteenth century, the German Karl Marx, whose name is chiefly associated with the theory of Communism. Marx's social ideology, however, developed from an historical study of the evolution of society, and of the economic relationship of classes within society. Although influenced chiefly by the work of figures like the philosopher Hegel, Marxist theory also possesses certain affinities with Darwinian theories of evolution, as, for instance, in the idea that the vitality of society is founded in the energies of the working class (the proletariat), which will adapt, survive and dominate since it provides the labour, while the middle class (the bourgeoisie) with the aristocracy will wither away as capitalism becomes obsolescent.

Marx developed his theory in the wake of the Industrial Revolution, which created an enormous working class that remained at the mercy of largely middle class industrialists, who controlled profitable sales, wages paid to labourers, hours of labour, the level of humanitarian concern (such as the provision of medical attention in the case of accident), and the like. Marx saw this latter class as motivated by the desire for profit, that is, wealth in excess both of actual costs of production and of actual need. In order to accomplish this objective, the capitalist industrialist required the worker to sell his or her labour at as low a value as possible.

Such a social and economic theory may seem rather remote from the concerns of literature. However, as Marxist theorists point out, the writing of books is also a mode of production, and it, too, is vulnerable to the sorts of forces that Marx envisioned in the factories and industrial cities that began to spread across Europe. To begin with, the author writes both to sell his or her work, and to reach a particular audience. Thus, the literary text becomes an economic commodity. Though there have been exceptions, most publishers are in the business of selling books profitably, and therefore are particularly sensitive to the market which they want to reach. When this fact is combined with a number of other social factors, such as the general level of education and of literacy; the diversity of political, social and other interests within the society; the existence and intersection of different ideas and ideologies; the modes of production and distribution of books; and so on, the individual manuscript is transformed from the simple product of its author's endeavours, and becomes instead a field in which different political, social and economic forces engage with one another.

In a culture, moreover, in which literacy is not widespread, those who are likely to purchase books will tend to belong to the same social class or range of classes. Inevitably, therefore, such readers will share similar points of view, political attitudes and social ideologies. Writing for this group of readers, the author is likely also to share its politics and ideology. In effect, therefore, the rest of the population is excluded from the individual text, which can start to exercise considerable power over the excluded population. Ideas are a potent force for change in a culture; and the forum for ideas, at least until the advent of the electronic media, has been chiefly in books, and in places where books are discussed, such as the university. This means that the literate and educated were reaching conclusions and making decisions for the illiterate and the uneducated: or, to put it more starkly, the few were leading the many.

In the realm of ideas, then, the intellectual may function like the capitalist industrialist: he or she controls the forces of persuasion which will inevitably affect the lives and quality of existence of the intellectual proletariat, the illiterate and the un- or undereducated. In political terms, this is dynamite, as we can see from the history of social revolutions across the entire world from the eighteenth century onwards. In most cases, such revolutions have been led or justified by small cadres of intellectuals whose points of view and whose ideas have affected the lives of millions. More recently, the development of means and modes of mass communication in a more widely educated society has meant that the control of ideas now can be seen as resting largely in the hands of those who control the mass media. The interests of this group are less likely to be governed by ideas alone, but rather to be influenced by political and commercial values.

Marxist approaches to literature are concerned to examine the text in terms of the historical conditions out of which it emerged. Literature is seen as part of a superstructure which includes other social institutions such as law, education, fashion, medicine, architecture, painting and so on, and which rests on a particular economic base consisting of the mode of production of a particular society. However, as Terry Eagleton and others are at pains to point out, the relationship of literature as a phenomenon in the superstructure to the economic base is not a simple, symmetrical one: it does not function as its mere mirror. To assume this is, in the first instance, to radically simplify the entire Marxist project in literary theory and criticism; and, in the second, it reduces literary analysis to a mere hunt through the text for references to industrial production, class differences, oppression of the proletariat, and the bourgeoisie, concluding with a judgement as to the text's worth on the basis of whether it predicts a working class revolution. This is the sort of reading which Frederick C. Crews guys in his collection of parodies of theory, *The Pooh Perplex*.[6]

It is the task of the superstructure not only to articulate the ideologies of the class which dominates the economic base, but also to *disguise* these as ideologies, to make social conditions and power relations among classes seem natural, or else, more simply, to render them invisible. Marxist theory raises the question as to what the function of literature is in this network of social and power relations. The French Marxist theorist Louis Althusser suggests that though the literary text is suspended within ideology, it is capable also of distancing itself from it:

> In doing this, art does not enable us to *know* the truth which ideology conceals, since for Althusser 'knowledge' in the strict sense means *scientific* knowledge ... The difference between science and art is not that they deal with different objects, but that they deal with the same objects in different ways. Science gives us conceptual knowledge of a situation; art gives us the experience of that situation, which is equivalent to ideology. But by doing this, it allows us to 'see' the nature of that ideology, and thus begins to move us toward that full understanding of ideology which is scientific knowledge. (Eagleton, *Marxism* 18)

According to Pierre Macherey, ideology may be perceived and comprehended through a careful reading of the literary text:

> a work is tied to ideology not so much by what it says as by what it does not say. It is in the significant *silences* of a text, in its gaps and absences, that the presence of ideology can be most positively felt. It is these silences which the critic must make 'speak'. The text is, as it were, ideologically forbidden to say certain things; in trying to tell the truth in his own way, for example, the author finds himself forced to reveal the limits of the ideology within which he

writes. He is forced to reveal its gaps and silences, what it is unable to articulate. Because a text contains these gaps and silences, it is always *incomplete*. (Eagleton 34–35)

In Macherey's theorising of the relation of the text to history, articulated through its ideological silencing, we see a point at which Marxist historicist theory touches on the philosophical and linguistic theory of deconstruction. Indeed, Marxist theory has been most influential upon other theories, especially feminist and gender theory. In the hands of later Marxist theorists, the Marxist approach has developed into a complex, often subtle exploration of the forces of power and ideology at work in society and in the literary text.

That exploration has not limited itself solely to the *content* of the text. For the Marxist, as for the New Critic and the Russian Formalist, form and content are not separable:

Form ... is always a complex unity of at least three elements: it is partly shaped by a 'relatively autonomous' literary history of forms; it crystallizes out of certain dominant ideological structures ... and ... it embodies a specific set of relations between author and audience. (Eagleton 26)

The form of a literary text, then, is not accidental, in the Marxist view: it is tied to and embodies particular historical facts as well as political and social relations.

This idea has not been easily and readily applied to poetic forms. Marxist theory by and large has preferred to examine those literary forms which directly address historical, political and social issues through their very material, and therefore may be assumed to be already saturated with ideological signification. Moreover, because these genres, namely, prose narrative and drama, appeal to larger audiences than does poetry, certain sociological and political inferences may be drawn concerning the nature of the ideologies articulated in works in these genres.

Poetry, by contrast, appears to present certain difficulties. Abrams defines 'lyric' as 'any fairly short, non-narrative poem presenting a single speaker who expresses a state of mind or a process of thought and feeling'.[7] The lack of narrativity, and the emphasis, in such a definition, on subjective processes such as mood, thought or feeling, might be thought to preclude a consideration of poetic form from the Marxist perspective.[8] Certainly some readers have been surprised — and have remained unconvinced — by a Marxist analysis such as Easthope's, which announces, in *Poetry As Discourse*, that 'poetic discourse since the Renaissance is ... co-terminous with the capitalist mode of production and the hegemony of the bourgeoisie as the ruling class. It is therefore a *bourgeois* poetic discourse' — a discourse, Easthope maintains, represented and maintained by a preference for iambic pentameter (24).

If we return to the example of Sidney's Sonnet 30, we can see that it is easier to conduct a Marxist analysis of the content than of the form. The references to political events suggest that the speaker has the social position that allows him to learn of such events. That he wishes to devote himself to his love for Stella, rather than concentrate on the matters of state being represented to him, gives an emphasis to those issues that implies the speaker's political importance. At the same time, this same fact excludes Stella from any political importance or activity: she is private, as opposed to the public matters with which the rest of the sonnet is concerned, and she represents an extension or a fulfilment of the speaker's sexuality. Whereas the other activities suggest political acumen and rationality and demand his intellect, she is the focus of the speaker's heart. In short, Stella as woman is excluded from the male realm of politics and the making of history.

At the same time, the poem is clearly addressed by a speaker to a recipient of the same social class as himself. Stella should be aware of her importance to Astrophil because she should be conscious of how significant are the matters that he wishes to abandon in favour of attending to his love for her. This implies a familiarity on Stella's part with such issues, or at least with the class of men for whom these are a responsibility. Also excluded, therefore, is a range of social classes below that of the noble courtier-statesman of the period.

This much information we can deduce from the content of the sonnet. What of its form? A study of the history of the sonnet during the English Renaissance would reveal several important issues, from the Marxist point of view. First, the number of variations on the sonnet form, from its originating Italian model through the French and English, attest to an interest at this time in miniature forms of art, as the popularity of painters like Nicholas Hilliard, the celebrated miniaturist, confirms. Miniatures, whether in verse or paint, are, first, the luxury of a class which has the leisure to produce and consume them, because they appreciate the fineness of artistry required by miniature representation. Smallness of scale demands a greater concentration in both producing and 'reading' such a form, and that concentration — since it depends on time freed for such activity — can be afforded only by a class with leisure.

Second, the function of the miniature was as an object of exchange. Lovers or spouses, or even monarch and courtier, would exchange miniature portraits of themselves, so that one would always have the likeness of the other close by. The purpose of the sonnet (whether we assume such a poem to have direct biographical reference or to be merely a fiction motivated by fashions in love poetry) was to provide a testimony of the speaker's feelings. Even if this was an asymmetrical exchange — there is little indication as to whether the beloved ladies also wrote sonnets to their lover-speakers — its function was essentially similar to that of the miniature portrait: it was, as it were, a verbal portrait of the speaker's emotions.

Third, the development of the sonnet form encouraged the use especially of the final couplet, but sometimes also the final tercet, as a device to wrap up the poem with a witty or sagacious remark. Such wit presupposes a certain kind of educated mind to appreciate it. Moreover, the frequent intertextual allusions in many Elizabethan sonnets to the works of various writers and philosophers, often non-English, point to a particular level of education in the writer, and its supposition also in the reader. Such education was likely to be found in the upper middle class, and in the nobility.

Fourth, sonnets were frequently written in sequences or cycles, rather than as individual poems. Such collections again imply sufficient leisure on the part of the poet to compose so many sonnet-units for his (such poets were usually male) cycle; also implied is a class of readers with the time to read them.

More more could be said about the sonnet, of course, but the above points allow us to conclude that it developed a form as among a class with a particular level of education and degree of leisure, namely, a nobility or gentry. This does not of necessity mean that *all* sonneteers were noblemen — Shakespeare, for instance, is assumed to be middle class — but it does imply that those poets who were sonneteers entered into a set of power and social relations which were essentially aristocratic in nature, for the initial consumers of this poetic form had defined the conditions by which it might develop. It is not, surprising, therefore, that Shakespeare's sonnets appear intended for a well-born reader like the young nobleman to whom most are addressed.

Marxist theory assumes a dynamic relationship between social conditions and the literary texts that a particular society produces. This is one of its great advantages over the older form of historicist theory, which inclines towards the more mechanical relationship of object and mirror. Marxist theory, however, is at heart a utopian theory: Marx's analysis of social relations, of relations of production and of social conditions are underpinned by a belief that history moves towards better and better conditions, and that eventually, in industrial society, capitalism will die of its own accord, and workers' socialism will replace it. This utopianism has sometimes affected the Marxist approach to texts, inviting evaluation of literature as 'good' or 'bad' according to whether it displays an evolutionary or revolutionary, that is, 'progressive', attitude.

The reason for such a concern in a literary theory is that Marxism holds to the belief that literature has the potential to transform society. This does not imply, however, a simple process by which a reader leaps straight from reading a novel or a poem to the defence of the ramparts against capitalist usurpation of workers' rights. Rather, the Marxist view maintains that because literature is part of the superstructure, and therefore reproduces the ideology of the social base, it has the potential to change that ideology, and hence the social base itself. By being able to distance itself from social ideology, and to open up gaps that permit — even invite — questioning of the ideology, literature is capable of subverting the latter, and thereby effecting change.

One theorist interested in the subversion of doctrines and ideologies was the Russian Mikhail Bakhtin. As we saw in the chapter on Russian Formalism, Bakhtin was for a while associated with the Formalist enterprise, but then disengaged himself from this school of theory on the basis of his political ideology and of his methods of analysis. Much interest has been shown in recent years in Bakhtin's writing, especially in his notions of *carnival* and of *dialogism*. Like many of the Marxist theorists and critics, Bakhtin's work is oriented particularly towards prose narrative.

The idea of carnival is explored in *Rabelais and His World*, in which Bakhtin shows that the mediaeval carnival was an officially sanctioned period in which the dogmas and doctrines, as well as the forms and the ideologies of official, dominant culture could temporarily be overturned. This resulted in activities that could technically be seen as blasphemous (parodies of religious rituals) or treasonous and socially subversive (parodies of kingship, inversions of master-servant roles, and the like). The phenomenon of carnival allowed, moreover, for a merging of categories that the ideologies of official culture kept separate: the serious and the ludicrous, the sacred and the profane, life and death, the rulers and the ruled, and so on. The advantage of carnival, according to Bakhtin, was that it reminded both the centres of official culture and the people at large of the arbitrary, conventional nature of the doctrinal divisions in the culture, of class distinctions, and of value judgments and differences.

It is important to note that Bakhtin considered Rabelais, the author of *Gargantua* and *Pantagruel*, the last of the writers and thinkers to engage authentically with carnival as an actual socio-cultural phenomenon. However, recent theoretical work using Bakhtin's ideas has extended the notion of the subversiveness of carnival to include writers later than Rabelais. The mimetic notion of literary carnival is associated with the idea of dialogism, which postulates that words are sites of conflict, since as signs they have been used not only in different, but opposed and contradictory, situations and contexts. Their meanings, therefore, lose definition and determination, and these signs become, rather, a locus in which cultural discourses and social forces are played out, in dialogue, as it were, with one another. Verbal texts, therefore, are places in which overt subscriptions to a particular doctrine or ideology are riven and disunified by the nature of the very material of which they are made. They become sites of ideological subversion.

We can see how this works if we return to an example we considered earlier, namely, war. Both the idea of war and its verbal sign are problematised when we realise that war has been glorified, sanctified and vilified. It has been experienced differently by soldiers at the front, and by those who remained behind. It has been experienced directly by soldiers, and indirectly by readers of war fiction and viewers of war films. It has been the occasion of triumph and joy, and of defeat and dejection. People have lost those close to them through war, and have grieved, or they have been reunited with them, and have rejoiced. Wars have been fought close to home, and in distant lands. These meanings of 'war' are not all mutually compatible. Moreover, the political significations attached to war are by no means easily determined. Was the suppression of pro-democracy supporters in Beijing in 1989 an internal matter of imposing law and order, or was it in fact an act of war-like aggression? The Chinese government argued the former; the West thought of it as the latter. Poems, therefore, which deal with war — the work of Wilfred Owen, or of Isaac Rosenberg, for instance — enter into a discourse about war which is filled with the tensions of the different significations and values relating to the idea of war itself, and which are webbed and meshed around the sign 'war'.

Bakhtin's notion of dialogism thus seeks to unite the semiotic nature and mimetic potential of language. It has much in common, on the one hand, with the Machereyan argument for gaps and silences in the text imposed by ideology, and, on the other, with the Derridean theory of deconstruction, which likewise argues that the verbal text contains the elements of its own subversion.

The notion of cultural discourse has also been important in the work of Michel Foucault, which has had considerable influence in recent years. Foucault's theory draws on Marxist and structuralist theory, among others, to argue that the members of a culture are enabled to perceive and 'think' events and ideas only in terms of certain powerful discourses in the culture. For Foucault, the eighteenth century marks the watershed for modern culture, for during this period certain intellectual, ideological, political and social developments took place which altered and shaped the ways by which we know. Social institutions like religion, education, medicine and the law imposed regularities (structures of pattern and control) which, on the one hand, committed culture to regarding as right, natural and inevitable certain practices and modes of perception, and, on the other, confirmed and strengthened the power of those institutions.

Thus, for instance, in a particularly influential study of human sexuality, Foucault argues that the body became a site, in the eighteenth century, for medical and legal discourses that essentially deprived the individual of the right to his or her body and its uses, by imposing normative practices and ways of knowing the body. Heterosexuality being defined as the norm, all other sexual orientations and practices were registered as deviant or abnormal rather than merely vicious or sinful, as the earlier discourse of religion had established. Members of the culture accused of such deviation could be publicly humiliated and ostracised, submitted to a 'curative' regimen, or even punished with imprisonment or death. Likewise, women who resisted the social and sexual roles imposed upon them by discourses which allocated power to men could be described as pathologically or psychologically hysterical, and exiled to hospitals, mental institutions, or, in other instances, prisons. In this way, human sexuality and its social dimensions are regulated and monitored by central powerful discourses, capable of delegating their power to individuals in the culture, or else withholding or withdrawing it from them.

Thus, a text as apparently familiar or innocent as a love poem actually participates in these cultural discourses of power in its articulation of the power relations between man and woman. Typically, the man, being active, loves, and thus controls the passive woman, who is beloved. The very idea of love itself is situated at the nexus of discourses of sexuality, social stability through marriage, preservation of property through descent of children, and so on. The simple 'I love you' of such poetry disguises extraordinarily complex and potent discourses functioning in the culture.

The difficulty with Foucault's theory is twofold. First, though the idea of the cultural discourses of authority and power is highly persuasive, these discourses are themselves fairly nebulous, manifesting themselves only indirectly through actual practices, so that their existence, identity and nature must be inferred. Second, the theory implies that these discourses are permanent and unchanging: though Foucault admits the notion of sites of resistance to the discourses of power, as a concept resistance implies guerrilla tactics, not wholesale revolution. It is, consequently, hard to know whether such discourses can be changed, and how, or, indeed, whether they ought to be changed. Implicit in Foucault's theorisation of discursive formations is the idea that change might depend in fact on some cataclysm occurring in the culture.

In addition, Foucault derives his observations principally from events and texts in seventeenth and eighteenth-century France, which was at the time a highly centralised monarchic autocracy. Conditions elsewhere in Europe were not always identical. In England, for instance, Parliament claimed a traditional right to moderate or refuse the monarch's demands and imperatives. Moreover, though intellectual activity in eighteenth-century Europe was certainly lively, it would be erroneous to suppose that *all* advances in philosophy, politics, science, industry and the rest occurred simultaneously with the dawn of the eighteenth century. Just as the Italian Renaissance is dated as taking place in the fifteenth century, but not in England until well into the sixteenth century, so the Enlightenment began earlier in some European cultures than in others. Indeed, some current scholarship along Foucauldian lines now pushes back to an earlier period than the eighteenth century the historical centre of gravity for particular discourses in the culture.

Foucault's work has been influential in the development of a recent historicist approach to literature, named the New Historicism or, sometimes, Neo-historicism. This theory employs the notion of discourse in order to detect in the culture of a specific historical moment certain patterns which are repeated throughout it in varying forms, ranging from political ideology and social practice to particular works of art and literature. The meaning of the literary text is thus seen to be embedded in a web of discursive formations which give it its meaning.

It might at first glance seem that New Historicism is simply the old historicism in another guise, that it seeks to find reflected in the literary text the historical events of its context. However, New Historicism draws on several other theories to investigate its object. In addition to a Foucauldian concern with the discourses of power and knowledge in a culture, New Historicism also employs current Marxist theory about the *production* of a text from particular political and socio-economic forces in the culture. Furthermore, structuralism also enters the New Historicist picture in that the latter seeks to identify and describe the systems of signification important to, and powerful in, a particular culture.

The consequence of this approach is a perception of the literary text as actually replicating in its own dynamics and structure those of the culture at large. Stephen Greenblatt's *Renaissance Self-Fashioning* is a model of this form of inquiry. In this book Greenblatt identifies as a potent discourse in the Renaissance the presentation of the self as a consciously produced object, and he shows how this pattern is to be found in the philosophical, political and literary life of the period.

It is thus no longer a question simply of the text's mirroring historical events. Rather, it is seen to be a molecular representation of the entire cultural organism, as it were. The text thus confirms the ideologies and dynamics of the culture at the same time as it reproduces them. At this point, we are a far cry from the historicist approaches of the nineteenth century.

Another, and fairly recent, outgrowth of the historical view of literature has been the study of post-colonial writing. This marshals the principles and reading practices of Marxist, Foucauldian and New Historicist theories to examine the body of writing by members of cultures which were formerly (and, in some cases, are still) colonies or dominions of European powers. Such literature typically deals with the after-effects upon the relevant culture of the dominant ideology and behaviour of the colonial power, as well as with the influence of the latter's language and literature upon native languages and literatures. A key text here is Edward W. Said's *Orientalism*, which explores the way in which the categories of 'the Orient' and of 'the Oriental' were constructed by Europe to define the exotic, the different and the Other. Thus, European ideals and practices could be defined as superior, normal and normative, those of the Orient, culturally inferior, deviant, even perverse (if not, indeed, perverted). The objects and terms of the discourse of post-colonialism, then, impinge on and include the issues of racism, and of the domination of one race by another, together with the rationale — emotive, philosophical, 'scientific' — for the privileging of one race over another.

From the perspective of post-colonialism, therefore, literary texts can be seen to define their readers prejudicially. Those for whom the literary text represents a normal reality are included as 'us'; those who must make an effort to grasp intellectually a culturally given state of affairs are excluded as 'others'. To take a simple example: Keats's ode 'To Autumn' presupposes a reader in the Northern Hemisphere. Readers in tropical countries — for instance, India, where seasons are distinguished by monsoonal periods — must try to apprehend the idea itself of autumn, which readers in Europe, say, may take for granted. Readers in the Southern Hemisphere likewise must learn to *invert* the cycle of the seasons. So, when Browning writes, 'Oh, to be in England/ Now that April's there ...' ('Home Thoughts, From Abroad' 1–2), the reader in Australia or New Zealand, say, must make the mental adjustment that April in the Northern Hemisphere is spring, not, as in the Southern Hemisphere, autumn. Such re-calculations of meaning are evidence of the exclusion or marginalisation of a culture by a Eurocentric, essentially colonialist way of thinking.

The poem has traditionally and conventionally been viewed as the subjective, personal statement of the individual poet. The various theories we have considered in this chapter emphasise the mimetic dimension of the literary text. Some, as we have seen, prefer to view the text as a document either of the poets' lives or times, whereas others, invoking complex and flexible notions of history, see the work as situated within a web of discourses of differing types. In any of its guises, the historicist approach resituates the poem, transforming it from a private utterance into the articulation of the culture's concerns and practices, thereby broadening the meaning potential in the poetic text.

Notes

1. A further point to be considered in this connection is the history of the reception of the text, an account of how a poem has been read by generations of readers: for, although the printed text may itself remain stable (allowing for possible manuscript variations, the history of the printed text, and the preferences manifested by a text's editors for particular versions of that text), the actual readings of a specific poem may display significant differences.
2. As with the term post-structuralism, the prefix 'post' signifies a conceptual relationship between Marxist theory proper and post-Marxist theory, rather than any evaluative idea that the latter supersedes the former because it is better or more recent.
3. See also Chapter 2, New Criticism.
4. I have placed quotation marks around 'correct' because the question of establishing a copy text is a difficult one. One can no doubt make a case for privileging a certain version of a manuscript or printed text by proving that errors occurred in the transmission of the text, at the hands either of copyists or of compositors. However, where variant versions exist which may well have been given authorial approval, whether explicit or implicit, or where a reading public has become familiar with a particular version despite its corruption through transmission, an argument can be made to preserve such variants and corruptions.
5. *The Poems of Sir Philip Sidney* (Oxford: Clarendon, 1962) 470. The text of Sonnet 30, cited above, is also drawn from Ringler's edition (179).
6. *The Pooh Perplex: A Freshman Casebook* (New York: Dutton, 1963) 15–26.
7. *A Glossary of Literary Terms*. 4th edn. (New York: Holt, Rinehart & Winston, 1981).
8. We might recall, however, that in Chapter 3 we considered the reverse possibility, suggested by Eugene Vance, that lyric poetry can in fact tell a story.

Suggestions for Further Reading

On Marxist Theory

Althusser, Louis. From 'Ideology and the State'. Rice and Waugh 54–62.

Balibar, Etienne, and Pierre Macherey. 'On Literature as an Ideological Form'. Young 79-99.

Benjamin, Walter. 'The Work of Art in the Age of Mechanical Reproduction'. *Illuminations*. 1955. Ed. Hannah Arendt. Trans. Harry Zohn. 1968. New York: Schocken, 1969. 217–51.

Bennett, Tony. *Formalism and Marxism*. London and New York: Methuen, 1979.

Eagleton, Terry. 'Conclusion: Political Criticism'. *Literary Theory* 194–217.

— *Marxism and Literary Criticism*. London: Methuen, 1976.

Easthope, Antony. *Poetry as Discourse*. London and New York: Methuen, 1983.

Forgacs, David. 'Marxist Literary Theories'. Jefferson and Robey 134–69.

Jameson, Fredric. *Marxism and Form: Twentieth-Century Dialectical Theories of Literature*. Princeton, NJ: Princeton University Press, 1971.

— 'Marxism and Historicism'. 1979. *The Ideologies of Theory. Essays 1971–1986, Vol. 2: The Syntax of History*. London: Routledge, 1988. 148–77.

Macherey, Pierre. *A Theory of Literary Production*. 1966. Trans. Geoffrey Wall. London: Routledge & Kegan Paul, 1978.

Marx, Karl. From *The Critique of Political Economy*. Rylance 202–3.

Selden, Raman. 'Marxist Theories'. 23–51.

Smith, Steven B. *Reading Althusser: An Essay on Structural Marxism*. Ithaca and London: Cornell University Press, 1984.

Williams, Raymond. 'Base and Superstructure in Marxist Cultural Theory'. Rylance 204–16.

— 'The Multiplicity of Writing'. Rylance 217–20.

Wilson, Edmund. 'Marxism and Literature'. Lodge, *20th Century Literary Criticism* 241–52.

On History and Historicist Approaches

Belsey, Catherine. 'Literature, History, Politics'. Lodge, *Modern Criticism* 400–10.

Greenblatt, Stephen. *Renaissance Self-Fashioning: From More to Shakespeare*. Chicago and London: University of Chicago Press, 1980.

Jameson, Fredric. 'Criticism in History'. 1976. *The Ideologies of Theory. Essays 1971–1986, Vol. 1: Situations of Theory*. London: Routledge, 1988. 119–36.

LaCapra, Dominick. *History & Criticism*. Ithaca and London: Cornell University Press, 1985.

— *Rethinking Intellectual History: Texts, Contexts, Language*. Ithaca and London: Cornell University Press, 1983.

McGann, Jerome J. 'The Text, the Poem, and the Problem of Historical Method'. Rylance 182–96.

Ransom, John Crowe. 'Criticism, Inc'. Lodge, *20th Century Literary Criticism* 228–39.

Ricoeur, Paul. *History and Truth*. Trans. Charles A. Kelbley. Evanston: North-western University Press, 1965.

Veeser, A. Aram, ed. *The New Historicism*. New York and London: Routledge, 1989.

Wellek, René. 'Literary Theory, Criticism and History'. Lodge, *20th Century Literary Criticism* 552–63.

White, Hayden. *Tropics of Discourse: Essays in Cultural Criticism*. Baltimore and London: Johns Hopkins University Press, 1978.

— *Metahistory: The Historical Imagination in Nineteenth-Century Europe*. Baltimore & London: Johns Hopkins University Press, 1973.

— 'The Value of Narrativity in the Representation of Reality'. *Critical Inquiry* 7 (1980): 5–27.

On Bakhtin

Bakhtin, M.M. *The Dialogic Imagination: Four Essays*. Ed. Michael Holquist. Trans. Caryl Emerson and Michael Holquist. Austin: U of Texas, 1981.

— *Rabelais and His World*. 1965. Trans. Hélène Iswolsky. 1968. Bloomington: Indiana University Press, 1984.

— *Speech Genres and Other Late Essays*. Trans. Vern W. McGee. Ed. Caryl Emerson and Michael Holquist. Austin: University of Texas Press, 1986.

Clark, Katerina, and Michael Holquist. *Mikhail Bakhtin*. Cambridge, Mass., and London: Belknap-Harvard University Press, 1984.

Morson, Gary Saul, ed. *Bakhtin: Essays and Dialogues on His Work*. Chicago and London: Chicago University Press, 1986.

Todorov, Tzvetan. *Mikhail Bakhtin: The Dialogical Principle*. Theory and History of Literature, Vol. 13. Trans. Wlad Godzich. Minneapolis: University of Minnesota Press, 1984.

On Foucault

Dreyfus, Hubert L., and Paul Rabinow. *Michel Foucault: Beyond Structuralism and Hermeneutics*. Chicago: University of Chicago Press, 1983.

Foucault, Michel. *The Archaeology of Knowledge*. Trans. A.M. Sheridan Smith. 1969. London: Tavistock, 1972.

— *The Foucault Reader*. Ed. Paul Rabinow. Harmondsworth: Penguin, 1986.

— *The History of Sexuality, Volume I: An Introduction*. 1976. Trans. Robert Hurley. New York: Vintage-Random House, 1978.

— *Language, Counter-Memory, Practice: Selected Essays and Interviews*. Ed. Donald F. Bouchard. Trans. Donald F. Bouchard and Sherry Simon. Ithaca, NY: Cornell University Press, 1977.

— 'The Order of Discourse'. Young 48–78.

— 'What Is An Author?' Lodge, *Modern Criticism* 197–210.

Hoy, David Couzens, ed. *Foucault: A Critical Reader*. Oxford: Blackwell, 1986.

Macdonell, Diane. *Theories of Discourse: An Introduction*. Oxford: Blackwell, 1986.

Merquior, J.G. *Foucault*. London: Fontana-Collins, 1985.

Sheridan, Alan. *Michel Foucault: The Will To Truth*. London: Tavistock, 1980.

On Post-colonialism

Ashcroft, Bill, Gareth Griffiths and Helen Tiffin. *The Empire Writes Back: Theory and Practice in Post-Colonial Literatures*. London: Routledge, 1989.

Miller, Christopher L. 'Theories of Africans: The Question of Literary Anthropology'. *Critical Inquiry* 13 (1986): 120–39.

Said, Edward W. *Orientalism*. 1978. Harmondsworth: Penguin, 1985.

7
Poetry and Gender

As Foucault defines it, a discourse is a way of talking about something that comes into being by virtue of that very act. What has come into being through the talk of feminist literary theory is the notion that poetry, and indeed all literature, is gendered. Feminist literary theory demonstrates that our socially given identities as feminine and masculine, and the differential access to social power and privilege those identities entail, shape the writing and reading of texts of all kinds, including poetry.

Discussing literature as gendered is something new. Received traditional and contemporary poetics are all gender-blind in one way or another. Traditional mimetic and expressionist theories emphasise the way in which literature represents a universal human nature, but its qualities upon closer examination are basically masculine ones. Theories such as New Criticism imagine the text as embodying a unified sensibility that transcends gender. Russian Formalist and, in their original statements, Marxist, structuralist, post-structuralist and deconstructionist theories think of writers and readers as defined by language, ideology and class, but not by gender. Classical psychoanalytic theories emphasise the processes of the unconscious in the production and reception of literature without reference to the description of differential gender formation provided by the theory. It is true that in each theory the feminine is often invoked, but always as a positive or negative metaphor for the meaning or experience which the theory says literature provides: moral truth, metaphysical insight, organic sensibility, the not-said of ideology, the repressed, *jouissance*,[1] and the like. Thus, in literary theory (as in most literature) the feminine becomes a figure of representation, an object that articulates a universal (masculine) subjectivity. What is left out in such figuring is the *difference* between women's and men's social and literary experience.

In the late 1960s and early 1970s, women began talking — about gender, about its relation to power and its relation to sexuality. This led on to its relation to textuality. In an important way, this talk was not new, though it may have seemed so at the time. Rather it was a return to a long debate within Western culture. Between 1300 and 1600, emergent humanism had struggled with the contradiction between its (Christian) idealisation of human nature and its (Christian) devaluation of women. The resulting *querelle des femmes* (quarrel of women) put woman into discourse both as 'problem' and as speaker. Thus, for example, Christine de Pisan defends the human — the moral and creative — capacity of women in *Le Trésor de la cité des dames* (1497; *The Treasure of the City of Ladies*, trans. 1984.

Later, at the end of the eighteenth and into the nineteenth century, the 'new liberalism' toiled over a similar contradiction, between its insistence on the democratic right of all human beings to liberty, equality and fraternity and its inability (implicit in the very word 'fraternity') to accord those rights to women in the same way as to men.

But women were not only spoken of; they also spoke. They argued passionately and forcefully against the customary and legal constraints that denied women the 'natural rights' liberalism claimed for all people. Mary Wollstonecraft's *A Vindication of the Rights of Women* (1792), Sarah Grimké's *Letters on Equality* (1838), Elizabeth Cady Stanton's Seneca Falls 'Declaration of Sentiments' (1848), Susan B. Anthony's two 'Address[es] to the New York State Legislature' (1854 and 1860), Harriet Taylor's (with John Stuart Mill) *The Subjection of Women* (1869), and Charlotte Perkin Gilman's *The Man-made World, or Our Androcentric Culture* (1911) are only a few examples of the vigour, complexity and richness of Anglo-American feminist talk in the nineteenth century. This talk in a different way also was conducted through literature, whose provinces nineteenth-century women invaded in such numbers that writers like Henry Lewis, Nathaniel Hawthorne and Henry James variously raised the alarm against 'scribbling women'.

Nor was the theorising of their bodies just talk. It was part of diverse political agitation to improve the social and economic conditions of women and to gain female suffrage. With women's enfranchisement, in 1902 in Australia, 1920 in the United States, and 1928 in Britain, what is sometimes called the 'first wave' of modern feminist theorising in the English-speaking world came to a close.

Of course, women did not stop talking about feminist issues. To take only a few exemplary instances: there were Virginia Woolf's meditation on a woman's literary place in *A Room of Her Own* (1928), Margaret Sanger's campaign against legal restrictions on women's access to birth control, and Simone de Beauvoir's existentialist explanation of women's subjection in *The Second Sex* (1949). However, such talk was for the most part marginalised or absorbed into other discourses

— those of literature, the family, philosophy and the like. Although the contradictions within liberal humanism between the doctrine of natural rights and the legal oppression of women appeared to have been resolved with women's enfranchisement, it took another epistemological break in Western social thought to call this seeming resolution into question. This put women, both as problematic subject and problematising speaker, back into discourse in a significant way.

This break in cultural consensus was related to the various post-World War II liberation movements — civil rights, sexual liberation and anti-Vietnam War activity in the United States; anti-establishment, including anti-nuclear actions in Europe; and independence movements in what came to be called the Third World. In different countries, in different contexts, with different theories, slogans and purposes, women variously enlisted for social action, only to find that the freedoms for which they marched did not necessarily include freedom from oppression on the basis of sex. In the formulation of radical American civil rights leader Stokely Carmichael, they found that the 'the only position for women in [such movements] is prone'. So, in a reprise of the experience of those nineteenth-century suffragettes whose alliance with abolitionists foundered when their agenda was strategically abandoned, many second wave politicised women withdrew their 'services' from the radical Left and began to talk about gender oppression, to (re)construct it as a discursive object.

A discourse emerges from the surfaces of other discourses and their institutions. As already noted, second wave feminism (especially in the United States) gathered up and resynthesised themes, concepts and values from Christian humanism, nineteenth-century liberalism and twentieth-century social and political liberation movements. Moreover, largely as a result of three generations of universal education, women were fitted for professional as well as domestic work (journalism, medicine, teaching, writing and the like). As a consequence of the evolution of the mass media, these women were also better placed than their predecessors for speaking from sites of authority. Betty Friedan's *The Feminine Mystique* (1963), which portrayed the oppression of suburban motherhood and wifedom, was a bestseller which was taken up and promoted through newspapers, magazines and television. The Women Against Pornography campaign of the 1970s made use of the media to promulgate the view that 'pornography is the theory, rape the practice'. In 1972, *Ms*, a mainstream (liberal) feminist magazine, was founded in the United States.

The academy, however, was an even more powerful, because less readily appropriated, site of speaking authoritatively, of speaking which is heard. In the field of literature, Kate Millett's pioneering exposition of misogyny in the works of D. H. Lawrence, Henry Miller and Norman Mailer, *Sexual Politics* (1970), originally a sociology dissertation, became a bestseller. The Modern Language Association, the professional body of English and language university teachers, formed the MLA Commission on the Status of Women (1970), out of which came the Female Studies series, seven volumes of course syllabuses and essays on women's issues. By the end of the 1970s, Women's Studies courses were an established (if ghettoised) feature of university programs. Professional feminist journals like *Signs* (1975), *Hecate* (1975) and *m/f* (1978) were brought out. Independent women's co-operatives and presses like Virago (1973) and The Women's Press (1977) were founded. In their wake, mainstream publishing houses began to promote feminist criticism and theory, frequently setting up monograph series devoted to these topics. By the end of the 1980s feminist literary discourse had moved to the centre of professional talk to such an extent that the strongest impression of the *Washington Post* reporter on the 1989 MLA Conference was the dominance of sessions on gender.

But centre-stage at the MLA is not necessarily a compelling indicator of success. For feminist literary theorising is not just a poetics, it is also a political enterprise. More precisely, it is a poetics whose politics are explicit rather than implicit. It seeks to understand the imbrication, the overlapping of gender, textuality and social power in order to change structures and processes that disadvantage women. As yet, the assumptions, discussions and perceptions that occur in a gender studies classroom have little place in the larger social world, or even in many other classrooms. Moreover, women both in the academic profession (as outside it) continue to be systematically paid and promoted less than their male nominal peers. Gender oppression is centre-stage in theory but has not fundamentally changed structures. This discrepancy within the literary profession, between the flourishing of feminist theorising and the real conditions of women's social and work experience, might be understood as a function of the fact that the idea for change always precedes change itself. More pessimistically, it can also be seen as resulting from the breakdown in theoretical consensus within the profession during the 1970s, a breakdown which has led to a proliferation of theories and theorising (as reflected in this book), and to an attitude of pluralistic acceptance. In these circumstances, the challenges of feminist literary theorising are diluted by its being just one of the many theoretical options available.

Such pluralism is also echoed within feminist literary theory. For not only are there several literary theories for feminists to draw on, there are also several feminisms, distinguished by their differing analyses of the mechanism of women's social oppression. What results is a variety of literary feminisms, including interrogations by lesbians and women of colour that extend the feminist concern with sexism to heterosexism and racism. This polyvocality within feminist literary theorising is, however, not viewed as a liberal compromise. Instead it is valorised (given value) as a necessary and productive heterogeneity, as a discourse, a debate about the implicit as well as the explicit ontological, moral, political and aesthetic assumptions that inform *any* theoretical enterprise. It is a valorisation that consciously ex-presses the awareness of being silenced, of being unheard because unadmitted to any authoritative site of discourse.

This polyvocality makes it difficult to represent literary feminism fairly in a brief introduction. However, across the various theoretical orientations there are common concepts and themes. Foucault regards such regularities, which he calls 'strategies', as one of the four condi-tions for the formation of a discourse. Two others were alluded to earlier: the formation of an object of theorising, that is, the gendered nature of writing and reading; and the availability of institutional sites from which to speak, for example, the academy. His fourth discourse is rhetoric or the style of statements, illustrated by the common feminist notion that such things as logical/linear argumentation and objective/universalising enunciation are masculinist, and use quite different rhetorical devices.

Three strategic concepts of feminist theorising are patriarchy, the sex-gender system, and phallocentrism. Recurring themes are silence, the mother, difference and sexuality/desire. In what follows, these three concepts are surveyed in order to demonstrate the regularities which identify the dispersed statements of literary feminism as a discourse, as opposed to a unified theory. Then three 'schools' or orientations of feminist poetics are identified, in order to indicate the play of these common themes across various feminisms, while at the same time preserving a sense of their differences.

Patriarchy, which literally means 'rule by the father', signifies any society in which males systematically hold the balance of power, and women are systematically subordinated to them. The feminist percep-tion is that our culture is fundamentally patriarchal. The doctrines of Judaeo-Christianity aver that we are all recipients of God's grace, that we are all his children — but also that women are more child-like than men. The principles of humanist and liberal individualism assert that we are all unique, moral and rational beings — but some of us are more so than others. Over the last century or so women have gained the right to vote, to hold property, to secure divorce, to receive child custody, to choose contraceptive devices and (less certainly) abortion, and to enter the workforce in significant numbers (if not significant positions). It is also true that the social status of (at least) Western, white, middle class women has improved since World War II.

Women's productive work, however, remains primarily located

in the poorer-paid service industries (cleaning, nursing, teaching, secretarial work and so on), or concentrated at the bottom of the professional salary scale (because, it is assumed, women will leave the workforce to follow a husband's career to a new place or to have children). At the same time, a woman's (dual-track) reproductive and domestic work — bearing and raising children, caring for the family — remains unvalued, unpaid and privatised. Perhaps least altered is women's sexuality and desire, which remain controlled and structured in ways that arguably serve men rather than women. These are the conditions under which most women live; they are, as the title of one of Juliet Mitchell's books puts it, 'woman's estate' — an estate bequeathed by patriarchy.

The mechanisms of women's estate, of their social oppression, are variously explained by the differing schools of feminist political (as opposed to literary) theory. Liberal feminism imagines that women are morally and intellectually equal to men, but lack equal opportunity of access to the social institutions that enable self-development. Marxist feminism concentrates on the way in which industrial capitalism organises women's labour, ensuring through its ideologies of family and motherhood that women willingly undertake the unpaid reproductive work of bearing and raising the next generation of workers, the similarly unpaid domestic work of caring for the current generation, and the poorly-paid productive work of providing a cheap labour force that can be moved in and out of the economy, as necessary. Radical and separatist American feminisms insist that the fundamental mechanism of women's oppression is neither a lack of opportunity, nor the manipulation of women's labour, but rather the social identities of feminine and masculine provided by society. Anglo-American psychoanalytic feminism describes how those identities are produced through child raising practices. Psychoanalytic Franco-feminism speculates on how they are produced through the operations of language both within society and within the psyche. This list of feminisms could be extended and elaborated. As it is, it reminds us of the important fact that a feminist poetics draws not just on aesthetic theories, but also on political ones that analyse those patriarchal social, ideological, political, legal and economic arrangements within society that exclude women from power, from the opportunities to control their own lives.

One of those arrangements is 'the sex-gender system', a term coined by the radical feminist Gayle Rubin in '"The Traffic in Women": Notes on a "Political Economy" of Sex' (in *Toward an Anthropology of Women*. Ed. R. Reiter, 1975). Though it is a concept that has been questioned and modified (see, for example, *Australian Feminist Studies*, 10, Summer 1989), it has been centrally influential and remains basically productive. In this phrase, the word 'sex' refers to the biological fact of femaleness and maleness, to the fact that there are two forms of the human species, identifiable by a difference in reproductive physiology. The word 'gender' refers to the social roles and psychological identities that we call 'feminine' and 'masculine', to that lived sense we have of what it means to be a woman or a man. Finally, the word 'system' points to those cultural processes and institutions whereby sex and gender are *linked*, so that sex-identity is understood to determine gender-identity: true women are feminine, true men masculine. The function of the sex-gender system, then, is to invest the biological fact of sex differences with the cultural meanings of femininity and masculinity. In post-structuralist terms, its function is to construct the body as a signifier of cultural meanings.

The belief that sex determines gender is supported by centuries of religious, philosophical, scientific and literary thought. As a result, it becomes commonsense for at least two reasons: first, because culture invests its meanings in something natural (in this case our bodies), such meanings appear to have been given by nature rather than to have been constructed by human activity. Second, because we are born into the system, it remains mostly invisible to us, and we learn to *be* feminine and masculine before we learn those words or their significance. In these ways, the cultural meanings created through the sex-gender system are, as a structuralist would say, *naturalised*, that is, disguised as facts of nature. However, the concept of the sex-gender system (in all its various theoretical inflections) insists that the connection between sex and gender is an arbitrary one, a product of culture. Nature gives the grounds and materials out of which gender is constructed: sexed reproductive organs and the reproductive processes of menstruation, ovulation, copulation, emission, conception, gestation and parturition. But culturally-guided human activity — that is, the sex-gender system — transforms these natural grounds and materials into the cultural forms of masculinity and femininity, together with the related ones of heterosexuality, romantic love, and motherhood. To paraphrase Simone de Beauvoir (295), we are born female and male, but we become feminine and masculine.

The radical feminist assertion that femininity and masculinity are cultural constructs is similar to the Marxist notion that they are myths or ideologies. The advantage of the Marxist formulation, however, is that it emphasises that such beliefs and values are not detached from social life, but rather are lived — are embodied in what we say and do, and have no other existence. Understanding this permits a more precise definition of the sex-gender system. This is that it consists of those social arrangements through which the ideological meanings of femininity and masculinity are inscribed in the bodies and minds of biological/psychological individuals, by means of specific practices and institutions, in order that certain social relations might be created and preserved. In feminist theorising, poetry is one of these institutionalised practices.

The notion of a sex-gender system provided by American radical feminist thought is in some ways congruent with the notion of phallocentrism within French post-structuralist and deconstructionist feminisms. However, whereas the sex-gender system model gives no precise idea of how representation or textuality functions as one of the social arrangements that produce gender identities, the latter approaches do so, in different ways. In *The Newly Born Woman*, Hélène Cixous invokes phallocentrism through a list of paired terms:

Activity/passivity,
Sun/Moon,
Culture/Nature,
Day Night,

Father/ Mother,
Head/heart,
Intelligible/sensitive,
Logos/Pathos.

Form, convex, step, advance, seed, progress.
Matter, concave, ground — which supports the step, receptacle.
Man
Woman   (63)

This list clearly articulates our culture's concept of gender difference, for we have no trouble recognising the final conclusion that Cixous draws. Additionally, it illustrates that those concepts are embedded in language and, by extension, representation and literature. Finally, it tells us about how femininity and masculinity are related to one another in that the meanings of each pair are oppositional: passivity is the absence of activity, nature is the absence of culture, and so on through the list, until one arrives at the notion that femininity is the absence of masculinity. In this way phallocentrism imagines masculinity and femininity as being complementary: if married, they produce a completed (masculine) whole.

The two terms of each pair do not, however, stand in a relation of reciprocity or equality. In each case the first term has priority and higher value: father is somehow greater than mother, and intelligible better than sensitive — and so on through the series, to the conclusion that man is somehow superior to, somehow more human (or indeed god-like) than woman. Thus, language and representation construct the relation between masculinity and femininity hierarchically: he is prior, completed; she is 'a certain lack of qualities', as Aristotle puts it, or an 'imperfect man', an 'incidental being', in St Thomas Aquinas' formulation.

These definitions of 'woman' by the great philosophers of ancient and mediaeval times are recalled for us by de Beauvoir in her introduction to *The Second Sex*. In that work, de Beauvoir uses existentialist terms for our culture's definition of the non-reciprocal and hierarchical nature of the relationship between masculinity and femininity. 'He' is subject or self; 'she' is object or not-self: that is, she is otherness. This alterity (otherness) of 'woman' has the effect of equating masculinity with humanity, and so our language conditions us to speak of mankind instead of humankind, and to use the masculine pronoun 'he' generically to represent both men and women. These usages point to a habit of thought, to ' phallocentrism', which means, literally, the centrality of the phallus, the symbol of male power. Man is central, woman peripheral; man is essential, woman complementary; man is prior and primary, and woman is secondary: de Beauvoir's 'second sex'.

The concept of the sex-gender system is primarily a sociological one, while that of phallocentrism is primarily philosophical and literary. The differences between these related concepts point to three main groupings within feminist literary theorising: American socio-historicism, French psychoanalysis/deconstruction, and British Marxism/socialism. (The geographical identities of each school indicate where each originated or holds sway; they do not suggest that Franco-feminism is not done by Americans or socio-historicism by British theorists, and so on.) American textual theory weds a liberal or radical politics to an historicised New Criticism. That is, it typically analyses the formal and semantic aspects of individual texts in order to uncover the ways in which they express a society's patriarchal values, or a woman-centred resistance and sensibility. The work of American critic Elaine Showalter illustrates this orientation. In *A Literature of Their Own* (1977), she uncovers a 'female literary tradition in the English novel' that expresses 'a subculture within the framework of a larger society', a subculture constituted by women 'unified by values, conventions, experience, and behaviors impinging on each individual' (12). She argues that this tradition has evolved in three stages: first, the feminine, in which women internalised phallocentric values and sought an equality with men; second, the feminist, in which women articulated their wrongs; and a third, the female, in which women's experience is regarded as an authentic subject of art. A later essay, 'Feminist Criticism in the Wilderness' (1981), undertakes to theorise this historically derived notion of a women's subculture by drawing on the concept of a 'muted group' in the work of Oxford sociologists Edwin and Shirley Ardener.

Similarly, in 'Towards a Feminist Poetics' (1979), Showalter moves to theorise the critical practice implied in the socio-historical approach by inventing two terms: 'feminist critique', which refers to gender-aware reading that uncovers patriarchal assumptions, stereotypes and values; and 'gynocritics', which refers to gender-aware reading that focuses on women who write from women's experience. Both methodologies react against what Mary Ellmann called 'phallic criticism' in *Thinking About Women* (1968), that is, criticism that adversely links women's writing to sex and gender, or ignores women writers altogether, or erases the specificity of women's experience and writing through universalising statements.

Taken together, Showalter's very influential pieces demonstrate the triple enterprises of American literary feminism: to recover women's writing that has been 'lost' through the operations of phallic criticism; to re-read from a woman-centred point of view the works phallic criticism has canonised (the 'images of women' approach); and to rejoice in and affirm woman-centred writing. It is an enterprise whose objectives are to contest and extend the literary canon, and give women — the muted group — an equal opportunity to speak their experience.

From the theoretical perspective of French feminism, American socio-historicism is empirical in a futile way: biologistic, essentialist and idealist (see, for example, Toril Moi's widely read *Sexual/Textual Politics* (1985). These terms of academic abuse point to the two feminisms' differing assumptions about the nature of the literary text, about authorship and about sexual difference. American critics like Showalter see the text as a *reflection* of a prior meaning or reality — of its author's prior historical experience (social, emotional, psychological, and so forth). French theorists or those like Moi, on the other hand, do not speak of discrete texts but of writing, of *écriture*. Drawing on Saussurean structuralism, Derridean deconstruction and Lacanian psychoanalysis, they assume that language constitutes human reality, that through language (or representation) culture inscribes social and sexual identities in the bodies and minds of biological/psychological individuals. A text, then, is not a reflection of prior meanings but rather part of the never-ending process of the *construction* of the meanings through which we live our lives. Meaning, therefore, does not originate in and flow from an 'author' who thereby transcends history; instead, conflicting cultural meanings flow through social beings who thereby reproduce and perhaps reinflect history. Put differently, French feminism replaces the essentialist, humanistic notion of the author as a psychologically coherent and metaphysically universalised 'self' with the post-structuralist notion of her as a psychologically disunified and metaphysically decentred 'speaking subject'.

French feminism gathered force in the 1970s, catalysed by the example of American feminists and the May 1968 insurgence against Gaullism and the French establishment. Very early, it defined its task to be the investigation of a 'sexual difference' which, like textual meaning, originates in and is constructed through language and writing. This focus is illustrated by the work of Luce Irigaray, which, like that of Hélène Cixous and Julia Kristeva, has been exported to the English-speaking world through anthologies like Elaine Marks' and Isabelle de Courtivron's *New French Feminisms* (1980), expositions like Toril Moi's *Sexual/Textual Politics* and the writings of Jane Gallop, Alice Jardine, Mary Jacobus and others.

In *Speculum of the Other Woman* (1974; trans. 1985), Irigaray reads the magisterial texts of Plato, Freud and other Western philosophers from the inside, not only for what is said but also for tone, contradictions, exclusions, repressions — for the 'blind spots'. Her interest is in the assumptions and central concepts of Western thought, and her purpose is to demonstrate that its 'representational economy' projects only one subjectivity and sexuality — a masculine one. 'Woman' supports this subjectivity and sexuality by functioning as an object of speculation and specularisation, as mystery and mirror. 'She' (as Cixous' list indicates) is represented in three ways, all of which repress her difference: either 'she' is just like man (human, rational, moral), in which case her specificity disappears, or she is unlike him (natural, irrational/intuitive, immoral/seductive), in which case she is somehow not fully human. Or she is man's complement (wife, mother, reflection), in which case she is a function of the masculine project of self-definition. Whatever variation of representation used, the result is that female difference and autonomy are erased. This is a representational system which, in Irigaray's terms, is driven by a 'desire for the same, for the self-identical, the self (as) same, and again of the similar, the alter ego and, to put it in a nutshell, the desire for the auto ... the homo ... the male dominates the representational economy' (26).

Within this economy, female autonomy and sexuality — female difference — are erased: the blind spot in the same old story of phallocentrism. The primary mechanism is the repression of the phallic or sexual mother. The mother is imagined as asexual, virginal, madonna-like, desirous only of a son whom she nurtures with milk and tears: such is woman's highest destiny and greatest good. This imagination is described in American feminism as the madonna/whore complex. But in Irigaray's analysis it is not simply a remediable element of masculine psychology. Rather, the elision of female sexuality and difference through the myth of the mother is the founding 'move' in the phallocentric project of self-definition, — and the foundation of its representational system. It pervades language and culture and is therefore internalised by women as well as men. Irigaray writes: 'Woman will therefore be this sameness — or at least its mirror image — and, in her role of mother, she will facilitate the repetition of the same, in contempt for her difference' (54).

Against this 'male imaginary', Irigaray invokes the possibility of a female imaginary — a representation of female difference, sexuality and autonomy. Only then, she argues, will it be possible to have a relationship *between* the sexes. Her method, like that of other French feminists, is writing — *écriture féminine*. Finding/writing the blind spots, contradictions and gaps through which women's discourse can be inserted into phallocentrism is the first step in this project. Beyond that there is the writing-into-being of women's sexuality, the sexualised mother and the autonomous woman. In attempting this, Irigaray's writing, with that of other French feminists, bends language and representation. She stages conversations, deploys non-linear argumentation, disrupts syntax, capitalises on ambiguity, has recourse to puns, irreverence and mockery, metaphorises the female body, imagines the mother-daughter relation as one between two sexualised beings, and invokes the divine as an image of female autonomy. Two of Irigaray's rhetorical devices — her use of female morphology (genital lips touching) as a metaphor for women speaking their specific experience, and her imagination of woman as god/dess-like — have sometimes been misread as biologism or essentialism (see *Sexual/ Textual Politics*). But this ignores her central analysis of how language and culture inscribe certain identities and sexualities in minds and bodies, and how this inscription silences women by erasing their difference. It also overlooks her commitment to the possibility of a 'female imaginary', the possibility of speaking a different female desire (plural, haptic,[2] non-goal-directed, fluid) and a different subjectivity (reciprocal, diffuse, mobile, open/ended). In short, it overlooks her understanding that any change in women's social, sexual and subject status requires a reinscription of femininity, the practice of *écriture féminine*.

French proponents of *écriture féminine* are more concerned with the making of poetry and literature than with a description of its nature or of a critical methodology. This last task has been taken up by Francophile American feminists. Thus, in her 'French Theories of the Feminine', (1985) Ann Rosalind Jones identifies four varieties of Franco-feminist criticism.[3] The first is deconstruction, the tracing of the logic of phallocentrism in a text. A second is hearing silences, reading between the lines for 'desires or states of mind that cannot be

articulated in the social arena and the languages of phallocentrism'
(99). A third is *écouter femme*, the empathetic and celebratory hearing
and representation of the feminine elements of a text. And, finally,
there is Franco-feminist close reading, one that draws the connections
between the text's formal structures and its underlying perception of
the feminine, but without the New Critical assumption that such
interpretation can be purely aesthetic, value-neutral, genderless. Perhaps the most useful Franco-feminist practice is one that synthesises
these approaches in a kind of double reading, simultaneously
deconstructive and (re)constructive.

British Marxist/socialist feminists are not convinced, however, that
the French feminist project is politically productive — or theoretically
sound. They agree that texts are part of a process of the social construction of meanings and subjectivities. However, they do not see
phallocentrism as a transhistorical tradition, nor writing as in itself
revolutionary. Instead, they define it as an aspect of ideology, and
argue that, as such, phallocentrism must be understood as in some
way related to the historically specific material conditions in which
women lead their lives. Just how they are related is the subject of
much debate and divergence within this school, but Michèle Barrett's
centrist position in *Women's Oppression Today* (1980) illustrates its main
concerns and orientation.

Barrett defines ideology as 'the processes by which meaning is
produced, challenged, reproduced, transformed' (97), and identifies
literature as an exemplary instance of it. In answering the question
of how ideology generally, and literature specifically, relate to material
conditions, she rejects classical economism, that is, the view that
each is an unproblematical reflection of economic or class relations.
On the other hand, she also rejects the post-structuralist Marxist
notion that ideology is an autonomous discourse, or that it is in itself
a material practice. Instead, she argues that ideology is *relatively*
autonomous: that is, that material conditions do not directly determine but do limit the range of what can be thought. Moreover, she
insists that, although ideology is invested in material practices, institutions and social relations, it is essentially a mental phenomenon
which has material *effects*. Gender, therefore, is not produced simply
by masculinist thought (Millett's male conspiracy, Irigaray's phallocentric tradition), but rather is a product of that thought as it relates
to the particular ways in which women's productive, reproductive and
domestic life is organised.

In this analysis, then, literature is just one of the ways in which
gender relations and gender ideology are produced and reproduced.
Woman's silencing is the effect of her relegation to the private,
domestic sphere, as well as the product of phallocentric representa-

tional economies. The myth of the mother is the effect of a division of reproductive and productive labour, as well as the result of the repression of the maternal/feminine within a masculine imagination of self. And the control of female sexuality occurs on the level of laws against contraception, of the provision (or not) of child care support, of judicial indulgence towards rape and wife battering, and so forth, as well as on the level of language and texts that represent women as desired but not desiring. For this reason a Marxist-feminist analysis requires attending to more than the text alone or to the writer in her historical situation (as in American socio-historicism). It entails understanding that what a writer can say and how she can say it are conditioned by: first, the general ideology of her period (as it relates to the general mode of production); second, by the aesthetic ideology of her period and the modes of literary production, distribution and reception; and, finally, by the author's individual and concrete experience of these conditions. In this model, literature is both a highly mediated reflection of a prior reality *and* a potent construction of it.

The debate among literary feminisms, only three of which are discussed here, has revealed some of the limitations of each kind. But it has also had the great advantage of encouraging feminist theorists to examine and articulate the assumptions of their practice, whether these are aesthetic, political, ethical or moral (about human nature). Just as profoundly, it has encouraged the same sort of examination and articulation in theorising generally: it has helped to make honest men out of gender-blind critics.

Feminist Theory in Practice

> I cannot live with You —
> It would be Life —
> And Life is over there —
> Behind the Shelf
>
> The Sexton keeps the Key to —
> Putting up
> Our Life — His Porcelain —
> Like a Cup —
>
> Discarded of the Housewife —
> Quaint — or Broke —
> A newer Sevres pleases —
> Old Ones crack —

I could not die — with You —
For One must wait
To shut the Other's Gaze down —
You — could not —

And I — Could I stand by
And see You — freeze —
Without my Right of Frost —
Death's privilege?

Nor could I rise — with You —
Because Your Face
Would put out Jesus' —
That New Grace

Glow plain — and foreign
On my homesick Eye —
Except that You than He
Shone closer by —

They'd judge Us — How —
For You — served Heaven — You know,
Or sought to —
I could not —

Because You saturated Sight —
And I had no more Eyes
And were You lost, I would be —
Though My Name
Rang loudest
On the Heavenly fame —

And were You — saved —
And I — condemned to be
Where You were not —
That self — were Hell to Me —

So We must meet apart —
You there — I — here —
With just the Door ajar
That Oceans are — and Prayer —
And that White Sustenance —
Despair —

(Emily Dickinson, No 640)

Because the occasions for Emily Dickinson's poems are, as here, so often left unstated, each invites being read in the context of her other poems and of her life. Traditionally, biographical critics stress the uniqueness of her life: her prosperous, nineteenth-century New England background; her unusually fine education; her experience of a distant father and an invalid mother; her intense friendships with women; her apparent erotic bereavement at about the age of twenty-two; her withdrawal from society by about the age of thirty, followed by a radical reclusiveness and the habit of wearing only white; and her writing in relative isolation some 1,775 remarkable poems, of which only 7 were published in her lifetime.

Feminist critics make less of the uniqueness of her life and relationships, and more of the ways in which her life and poetry were shaped by the constraints of sexual and gender norms of her society. In the case of this poem, feminist critics are not so much concerned that it provides some evidence that the Reverend Charles Wadsworth was the 'lover' (actual or a creation of her desire) whose loss motivates her poems. Rather they emphasise how these poems articulate desire and preserve it, despite constraint and loss.

Though hardly the sole focus of feminist criticism, Dickinson's love poems are given new focus in it, for they pose direct questions of gender and sexuality. There are some 90 or so poems to or about a woman, and many hundreds to or about a male and/or — as in this poem — an other whose sex cannot be determined. Together these poems present a four-part narrative: an unspecified erotic bereavement; pain that disorients; death-like despair; and accommodation achieved through the choice of suffering over not-feeling, the solace of nature, the affirmation of self-selected solitude, the celebration of desire that persists in spite of loss, and — especially — the writing of poetry.

'I cannot live with You — ' forms a part of this narrative. Its absent occasion is an erotic loss protested in the first line: 'You' are 'Life' and someone or something or even 'You' have taken away you/life/love. It is as though a communion cup, a holy thing, has been locked away by a sexton, a maintainer of church property and grave-digger. You/life/love/communion cup are 'Behind the Shelf' — sitting on the shelf, hidden behind closed doors. The grave-digger handles 'Our' lost life as though it were 'His', as though he were a housewife putting away cracked, broken, unwanted 'Porcelain'.

Thus, the religious imagery of the first three stanzas insists, Donne-like, upon the holiness of human love, and initiates the poem's metaphoric argument for the transcendence of desire. At the same time, the domestic imagery (whose disparateness is also reminiscent of the Metaphysical style), suggests the homeliness of such love and implies its power to nurture and define (an implication picked up in the poem's later image of a 'homesick' Eye/I bereft of the the sight and presence of the beloved). And, finally, this intertwined imagery conveys the rage and pain when such love is 'Discarded' and devalued.

But the first line is not only a protest against loss, but also an assertion of a choice: I cannot/will not live with you. This assertion flows from the conclusion of the poem's argument. For, again in a Metaphysical manner, this poem is structured like a logical argument. The proposition is stated in the opening line and developed in the first three stanzas; four reasons in defence of it are presented (in stanzas four to five, six to nine, ten and eleven), and the conclusion is given in the final stanza. Thus, the logic of the poem is not only linear but also circular, for the compacted images of the conclusion give rise to the abstract assertion of the opening line. Moreover, the four reasons-in-defence draw their imagery from the Christian catalogue of the four last things: death, resurrection and judgement, heaven, and hell. Thus, the very structure of the poem suggests the apocalyptic quality of the speaker's pain, despair and desire.

The presiding metaphor of the first reason in defence (stanzas four and five) is death, a thematisation prepared for by the loss-of-life and grave-digger imagery of the opening. This is the first step in the poem's conversion of an enforced condition to an elected one, and it is signalled by the use of the subjunctive verb 'could not'. Like the 'cannot' of the first line, it carries the double meaning of being prevented and of choosing, but now the situation is hypothetical. The reasoning of these lines is this: to live with 'You' would inevitably lead to a moment when one of us dies; neither of us could bear such loss and separation ('I could not ... You — could not — '); therefore, I cannot/will not live with you. It is a logic that distances an unbearable present pain, an emotional loss that feels like physical death, by transposing it to the future and by projecting the speaker's feelings onto the beloved ('I could not ... You — could not — ').

The eschatological structure, that pertaining to the four last things, continues in the next four stanzas, where reasons for choosing not to live with the beloved are developed through images of resurrection and judgement. Once more the argument is that the impossibility of a future event — resurrection — prevents the possibility of a present one — living together. Resurrection is impossible because if alone at resurrection, the speaker's memory of the beloved's face would make that of Jesus 'plain' and 'foreign'. If with the beloved, on the other hand, the latter's face would eclipse that of Jesus. Thus both beloved and love are blasphemously measured: 'You' are to me light and Christ-like sun, a 'Grace' prior to Christ, a 'Home' more excellent than 'Paradise'. Like the enforced choice of the opening, this blasphemy is both compelled and volitional: 'Because You saturated Sight — ,' I 'could not' have chosen 'Heaven' — as you have. Yet nothing is confessed other than the divinity of the beloved and the transcendence of loving. Through such idealising and eternalising tropes, present loss and pain are again distanced and defended against.

As a result, judgement itself is called into question. 'They'd judge Us — How — ' suggests that only the *fact* of judgement is certain. Who will judge is obscured in so far as the conceit, or extended metaphor, suggests Christ, but the pronoun suggests simply hostile others. And the question 'How — ' suggests the possibility that such love might not be condemned, and so might not be blasphemous. In any case, the reasons of stanzas ten and eleven set aside both social and divine constraint, as irrelevant. Here, two of the four possible results of the lovers facing the last judgement together are imagined: those in which the two lovers would be differently judged, and so 'condemned' to eternal separation. This in itself 'were Hell to Me — '. And so again the poem projects a present loss into the future, and thereby wins a small psychic space in which there is some choice: 'I cannot live with You — ,' since living, dying and entering eternity together might well lead to unendurable separation.

It is just such separation, such Hell, that the poem denies. For to live apart is not to be apart, if one chooses to do so, or if love transcends death, judgement, heaven and hell. This is the conclusion signalled by the 'So' of the last stanza's opening, and developed through the oxymoron 'We must meet apart — ,' and the surreal image of a 'Door ajar/ That Oceans are — .' It is a conclusion that is been hard fought, and yields some degree of control and self-affirmation, some way to preserve desire. In this manner 'Despair' is converted into 'that White Sustenance — ' that serves as prayer, or hope might serve were the bereavement less apocalyptic. This final image, with its allusion to both the bridal garment and the shroud, thus invokes both a loss that is past bearing and one that is transformed through 'argument', words, poetry.

In choosing passion (however unreciprocated) and poetry (however unpublished) over wifedom and motherhood, Emily Dickinson led a life which her society (like ours) regarded as 'unnatural' — unfeminine. She no doubt, then, experienced what Vivian R. Pollak has called 'the anxiety of gender' (*Dickinson: The Anxiety of Gender*, 1984). Indeed, a case could be made for understanding both her reclusiveness and the elliptical quality of the poems as a response to the conflict between the choices she made and the ones her society dictated. Her responsive strategy was one described in another of her poems: 'Tell all the Truth but tell it slant — ' (No 1,129). It is a truth which is obscured by criticism and anthologising that does not take gender into account. Such criticism dwells on the moral impulse of

Dickinson's poetry, calls attention to the nature poems, and describes her as a religious poet. Curiously, it does not emphasise the number and intensity of love poems like this one.

Notes

1. *Jouissance* is a French term signifying 'pleasure', in particular, 'sexual pleasure, bliss'. Roland Barthes distinguishes between *plaisir* (pleasure) and *jouissance* (bliss) in *The Pleasure of the Text* (1973), trans. Richard Miller (New York: Hill and Wang, 1975). In the 'Note on the Text' in this work, Richard Howard observes: 'Pleasure is a state, of course, bliss (*jouissance*) an action, and both of them, in our culture, are held to be unspeakable, beyond words' (vi).
2. Haptic: pertaining to the sense of touch (the reference here is to haptic pleasure, as opposed to visual pleasure, often identified as typically masculine).
3. See *Making a Difference*. Ed. G. Greene and C. Kahn, London: Routledge, 1985.

Suggestions for Further Reading

(These suggestions include only post-World War II feminism, not all those cited in the chapter.)

On American Socio-historical Theory

Chodorow, Nancy. *The Reproduction of Mothering: Psychoanalysis and the Sociology of Gender*. Berkeley: University of California Press, 1978.

Eisenstein, Hester. *Contemporary Feminist Thought*. Boston: G.K. Hall, 1983.

Ellman, Mary. *Thinking About Women*. New York: Harcourt, Brace and World, 1968.

Evans, Mari, ed. *Black Women Writers, 1950–1980: A Critical Evaluation*. New York: Anchor, 1984.

Faderman, Lillian. *Surpassing the Love of Men: Romantic Friendship and Love Between Women from the Renaissance to the Present*. New York: William Morrow, 1981.

Flynn, Elizabeth A. and Patrocinio P. Schweickart, eds. *Gender and Reading*. Baltimore and London: Johns Hopkins University Press, 1986.

Friedan, Betty. *The Feminine Mystique*. New York: Norton, 1963.

Gilbert, Sandra M., and Susan Gubar. *The Madwoman in the Attic: The Woman Writer and Nineteenth-Century Literary Imagination*. New Haven, Conn.: Yale University Press, 1979.

— eds. *Shakespeare's Sisters: Feminist Essays on Women Poets*. Bloomington: Indiana University Press, 1979.

Juhasz, Suzanne, ed. *Feminist Critics Read Emily Dickinson*. Bloomington: Indiana University Press, 1983.

The Lesbian Issue. Signs 9, Summer 1984.

Millett, Kate. *Sexual Politics*. Garden City, New York: Doubleday, 1970.

Olsen, Tillie. *Silences*. New York: Delacorte, 1979.

Rich, Adrienne. *On Lies, Secrets, and Silence: Selected Prose 1966–1978.* New York: Norton, 1979 (lesbian feminist criticism).

Showalter, Elaine, ed. *Feminist Criticism: Essays on Women, Literature, and Theory.* New York: Pantheon, 1985 (includes her 'Toward a Feminist Poetics' and 'Feminist Criticism in the Wilderness'.)

— *A Literature of Their Own: British Women Novelists from Brontë to Lessing.* Princeton, NJ: Princeton University Press, 1977.

Pollak, Vivian R. Dickson. *The Anxiety of Gender.* Ithaca: Cornell University Press, 1984.

— ed. *Speaking of Gender.* London: Routledge, 1989.

Stetson, Erlene. *Black Sister: Poetry by Black American Women, 1764–1980.* Bloomington: Indiana University Press, 1981.

Todd, Janet. *Feminist Literary History.* New York: Routledge, 1988.

Tong, Rosemarie. *Feminist Thought: A Comprehensive Introduction.* Boulder, Colorado: Westview, 1989.

Walker, Alice. *In Search of Our Mothers' Gardens: Womanist Prose.* New York: Harcourt Brace Jovanovich, 1983 (black feminist criticism).

On British Feminist Socialism/Marxism

Belsey, Catherine. *Critical Practice.* London: Methuen, 1980.

Barrett, Michèle. *Women and Writing.* London: Women's Press, 1979.

— *Women's Oppression Today: Problems in Marxist Feminist Analysis.* London: Verso, 1980.

Coward, Rosalind. *Patriarchal Precedents: Sexuality and Social Relations.* London and Boston: Routledge & Kegan Paul, 1983.

— *Female Desire.* London: Paladin, 1984.

Delany, Sheila. *Writing Women: Women Writers and Women in Literature, Medieval to Modern.* New York: Schocken, 1984.

Kaplan, Cora. 'Pandora's Box: Subjectivity, Class and Sexuality in Socialist Feminist Criticism'. *Making a Difference.* Ed. G. Greene and C. Kahn. London: Routledge, 1985.

— *Sea Changes: Culture and Feminism.* London: Verso, 1986.

Keohane, Nannerl O., Michelle A. Rosaldo and Barbara C. Gelpi, eds. *Feminist Theory: A Critique of Ideology.* London: Harvester, 1981.

Kuhn, Annette and Annemarie Wolpe, eds. *Feminism and Materialism: Women and Modes of Production.* London: Routledge & Kegan Paul, 1987.

MacKinnon, Catharine. 'Feminism, Marxism, Method, and the State: An Agenda for Theory'. *Signs* 7 (1982): 515–44.

Mitchell, Juliet. *Women: The Longest Revolution.* New York: Pantheon, 1984.

— *Psychoanalysis and Feminism: Freud, Reich, Laing, and Women.* New York: Pantheon, 1974.

— *Women's Estate.* New York: Pantheon Books, 1971.

Robinson, Lillian S. 'The Norton Anthology of Literature by Women: Is There a Class in This Text?' *Tulsa Studies in Women's Literature* 5 (1986): 289–302.

— *Sex, Class, & Culture.* 1978. New York: Methuen, 1986.

Rubin, Gayle. 'The Traffic in Women: Notes on the "'Political Economy" of Sex'. In *Toward an Anthropology of Women.* Ed. Rayna Reiter. New York: Monthly Review Press, 1978: 157–210.

Sargent, Lydia, ed. *The Unhappy Marriage of Marxism and Feminism: A Debate on Class and Patriarchy.* London: Pluto Press, 1981.

Wolff, Janet. *The Social Production of Art.* London: Macmillan, 1981.

On French Feminisms

De Beauvoir, Simone. *The Second Sex.* Trans. and ed. H. M. Parshley. Harmondsworth: Penguin, 1972.

Cixous, Hélène. 'Castration and Decapitation'. Trans. A. Kuhn. *Signs* 7 (1981): 41–55.

— 'The Laugh of Medusa'. 1975. Trans. K. Cohen and P. Cohen. *Signs* 1 (1976): 875–93.

— and Catherine Clément. *The Newly Born Woman.* 1975. Trans. B. Wing. Manchester: Manchester University Press, 1985.

Felman, Shoshana. *Writing and Madness (Literature/Philosophy/Psychoanalysis).* Ithaca, NY: Cornell University Press, 1985.

Feminist Readings: French Texts, American Contexts. Yale French Studies 62 (1981).

Gallop, Jane. *The Daughter's Seduction: Feminism and Psychoanalysis.* Ithaca, NY: Cornell University Press, 1982.

— *Reading Lacan.* Ithaca, NY: Cornell University Press, 1986.

Grosz, Elizabeth. *Sexual Sub Aersions: Three French Feminists.* Sydney: Allen & Unwin, 1989.

Irigaray, Luce. *Divine Women.* Trans. S. Muecke. Sydney: Local Consumption Occasional Papers 8.

— *The Sex Which is Not One.* 1977. Trans. C. Porter, with C. Burke. Ithaca, NY: Cornell University Press, 1985.

— *Speculum of the Other Woman.* 1974. Trans. G.C. Gill. Ithaca, NY: Cornell University Press, 1985.

Jardine, Alice. *Gynesis: Configurations of Woman and Modernity.* Ithaca, NY: Cornell University Press, 1981.

Jones, Ann Rosalind. 'French Theories of the Feminine.' In *Making a Difference: Feminist Literary Criticism.* Ed. G. Greene and C. Kahn. London and New York: Routledge, 1985.

Kristeva, Julia. *Desire in Language: A Semiotic Approach to Literature and Art.* 1977. Trans. L. S. Roudiez, A. Jardine and T. Gora. New York: Columbia University Press, 1982.

— *The Kristeva Reader.* Ed. Toril Moi. Oxford: Blackwell, 1986.

— *Powers of Horror: An Essay on Abjection.* 1980. Trans. L. S. Roudiez. New York: Columbia University Press, 1982.

— *Tales of Love.* 1983. Trans. L. S. Roudiez. New York: Columbia University Press, 1987.

L'écriture féminine. Contemporary Literature 24 (Summer 1983).

Marks, Elaine and de Courtivron, Isabelle, eds. *New French Feminisms: An Anthology.* Amherst: University of Massachusetts Press, 1980.

Mitchell, Juliet, and Jacqueline Rose, eds. *Feminine Sexuality: Jacques Lacan and the École Freudienne.* New York: Norton, 1982.

Miller, Nancy K., ed. *The Poetics of Gender.* New York: Columbia University Press, 1986.

Moi, Toril, ed. *French Feminist Thought*. Oxford: Blackwell, 1986.
Moi, Toril. *Sexual/Textual Politics: Feminist Literary Theory*. London: Methuen, 1985.
Rose, Jacqueline. *Sexuality in the Field of Vision*. London: Verso, 1986.
Spivak, Gayatri. *In Other Worlds: Essays in Cultural Politics*. London: Methuen, 1987.

Some Current Feminist Journals

Australian Feminist Studies; camera obscura: A Journal of Feminism and Film Theory; Diacritics; Feminist Issues; Feminist Review; Feminist Studies; Genders; Hecate: A Women's Interdisciplinary Journal; Journal of Women's Studies in Literature; m/f: A Feminist Journal; Sage: A Scholarly Journal on Black Women; Signs: Journal of Women in Culture and Society; Sinister Wisdom: A Journal of Lesbian/Feminist Experience; Tulsa Studies in Women's Literature; Women's Studies.

8

The Poem in Theory

In his article 'Normal Circumstances, Literal Language, Direct Speech Acts, the Ordinary, the Everyday, the Obvious, What Goes without Saying, and Other Special Cases',[1] Stanley Fish, tells the following anecdote about

> a sign that is affixed in this unpunctuated form to the door of the Johns Hopkins University Club:
>
> PRIVATE MEMBERS ONLY
>
> I have had occasion to ask several classes what that sign means, and I have received a variety of answers, the least interesting of which is, 'Only those who are secretly and not publicly members of this club may enter it.' Other answers fall within a predictable and narrow range: 'Only the genitalia of members may enter' (this seems redundant), or 'You may only bring your own genitalia,' or (and this is the most popular reading, perhaps because of its Disney-like anthropomorphism) 'Only genitalia may enter.' In every class, however, some Dr Johnson-like positivist rises to say, 'But you're just playing games; everyone knows that the sign really means, "Only those persons who belong to this club may enter it."' He is of course right. (274–75)

Fish is arguing for a particular theory of the reader's response to the literary text, and remarks about this story that

> Constituting *their* [the students'] perception is not the knowledge of what to do with signs on faculty club doors but the knowledge of what to do with texts written on blackboards by professors of English literature. That is, professors of English literature do not put things on boards unless they are to be examples of problematic or ironic or ambiguous language. Students know that because they know what it means to be in a classroom, and the categories of

142

understanding that are the content of that knowledge will be organizing what they see before they see it. (277)

Fish's point here is an important one, for it bears on the discussion of literary theory and its applications, both in this book and in general practice. When we read a literary text, the context and circumstances of that reading include certain pertinent expectations of the text, and of the kind of meaning we propose to make in it. We are less likely, when reading a fantasy novel on a train, to invoke the apparatus of the theory of deconstruction, say, than when we are instructed by a teacher to write an essay on a set text in a course — even if that text happens to be the same fantasy novel. In other words, the way in which theory underpins how we read depends as much on the circumstances under which we read as it does on the nature of the text itself.

So, when a teacher asks a group of students, 'What does this poem mean?', the students know, from experience and practice, that they are not necessarily being invited to say what the poem means immediately to *them*. Rather, the situation requires students to route the poem's meaning through some stated or unstated theoretical grid, often conceived as what the teacher expects them to say about the text, and to produce a meaning that is not only coherent and plausible, but one that acknowledges the authority and power of that theoretical grid.

As we noted in the first chapter, even when a reading is ostensibly 'natural', there is still a theory at work behind it. After all, reading as a physical activity itself is not natural: it must be learned. And that reading in particular ways can be taught and learned is evidenced by the long-standing existence, first, of literary 'cribs' to specific works such as the Monarch Notes, Cliff Notes, Barron Notes, and so on. The recent expansion into this market of various prestigious publishers, such as Cambridge University Press (Landmarks in Literature Series), Macmillan (How to Study Literature Series — the series title in itself significant), and Blackwell (Rereading Literature Series) confirms that this is so. The difference between the first and second categories of work is that the former tends towards a fairly mechanical New Critical approach, whereas the latter applies more recent theories to the reading of literary texts.

The mere comparative difficulty of poetic language suggests that poetic texts are necessarily read less naturally than works in prose. It is the task of one kind of theory to smooth over the effort of reading such texts, and to make it seem effortless and natural. Because literature departments in schools and, to a large extent, in universities are in the business of making texts more, rather than less, accessible to students, this type of theory will tend, first, to be widespread, and second, to have a certain traditionalism about it. Its very ubiquity in both time and place makes it invisible, and hence apparently 'natural'. Such, indeed, until relatively recently has been the status of Anglo-American New Criticism, with which our exploration of theory and poetry commenced.

Other kinds of theory seek, by contrast, to destabilise or, in the words of Russian Formalist theory, to 'roughen' the approach to the literary text. These theoretical positions tend, therefore, to estrange the way in which we deal with poetic texts, and to objectify the relevant theories: that is, to make them visible and, as it were, 'unnatural'. It is in this objectification of theory that some of the difficulty of these approaches lies. On the one hand, it refuses to transform theory simply into a method and a tool. On the other, it does not — as in the case of deconstruction — guarantee the final transparency of the poetic text.

Theory is the definition and description of reading practice. Thus, for instance, if we were to formulate the ways in which pleasure might be obtained from reading, we would be theorising a particular practice of reading. But theories may also in turn define and direct reading practices. Knowing about structuralism or about the New Historicism *as theories* can affect the way in which we go about reading texts in the future. This is especially important in an era like the present, when theories burgeon and proliferate, and academics and their students may divide into factions governed by the politics of the particular theory espoused. In other words, literary theory has become more than a merely 'theoretical' way of approaching a text: it is capable of antagonising some critics, exposing the political affiliations of others, and dividing and alienating whole classes, departments or faculties.

Each of the theories discussed in this book has its own difficulties, advantages and weaknesses, not all of which are purely literary and academic. But each also offers a different way of making sense — different senses — of the text. Some of these inevitably carry a certain political weighting and orientation. The poem, in theory, thus becomes potent not only of meaning, but also of value, whether literary, social or political.

Notes

1. *Critical Inquiry* 4 (1978): 625–44. Reprinted in *Is There a Text in This Class? The Authority of Interpretive Communities* (Cambridge, Mass. and London: Harvard University Press, 1980) 268–92. References in the text cite the latter source.

Index